# So You Want
# to Be a
# STAY-
# AT-HOME
# MOM

Cheryl
Gochnauer

**InterVarsity Press**
Downers Grove, Illinois

InterVarsity Press
P.O. Box 1400, Downers Grove, IL 60515
World Wide Web www.ivpress.com
E-mail· mail@ivpress.com

InterVarsity Press® is the book-publishing division of InterVarsity Christian Fellowship/USA®, a student movement active on campus at hundreds of universities, colleges and schools of nursing in the United States of America, and a member movement of the International Fellowship of Evangelical Students For information about local and regional activities, write Public Relations Dept , InterVarsity Christian Fellowship/USA, 6400 Schroeder Rd., P.O. Box 7895, Madison, WI 53707-7895

Cover photographs Britt Erlanson/Image Bank; Ross Whitaker/Image Bank

ISBN 0-8308-1922-3

Printed in the United States of America ♾

**Library of Congress Cataloging-in-Publication Data**

Gochnauer, Cheryl, 1958-
   So you want to be a stay-at-home mom/Cheryl Gochnauer.
     p     cm
   Includes bibliographical references.
   ISBN 0-8308-1922-3 (alk paper)
   1 Mothers—United States   2 Housewives—United States
  3 Motherhood—United States.   I Title
HQ759 G56    1999
306 874'3—dc21                              99-15064
                                                      CIP

| 21 | 20 | 19 | 18 | 17 | 16 | 15 | 14 | 13 | 12 | 11 | 10 | 9 | 8 | 7 | 6 | 5 | 4 | 3 | 2 | 1 |
|----|----|----|----|----|----|----|----|----|----|----|----|---|---|---|---|---|---|---|---|---|
| 16 | 15 | 14 | 13 | 12 | 11 | 10 | 09 | 08 | 07 | 06 | 05 | 04 | 03 | 02 | 01 | 00 | 99 | | | |

When I was pregnant with my first child,
Becky Walker was the conscientious working mom
stationed at a nearby desk.
As my baby grew inside me,
I watched Becky conceive her own plan
for spending more time
with her young daughters.
By the time Karen was born,
Becky had broken free of her cocooned cubicle
and transformed into a vibrant
stay-at-home mom.

Thanks, Beck-o, for modeling
how wonderful the life of a stay-at-home mom can be.
You were right.
This book is dedicated to you.

# Acknowledgments

A couple of years ago, I stepped to the window overlooking a friend's garden. The words "I have found the Promised Land, and it's in my own backyard" flashed through my head. Struck with inspiration, I raced home to my computer and started writing an article targeting working mothers who wanted to quit so they could spend more time with their children.

With my "So You Want to Be a Stay-at-Home Mom" article in hand, I headed to the local newspaper office. The story ran as a four-part series and generated positive letters and phone calls to *The Lee's Summit Tribune*. Just as I had suspected, lots of mothers were struggling with the issue of whether or not to work full time. And those who were at home were feeling underappreciated by society in general.

"Would you be interested in a monthly column to encourage stay-at-home moms?" I asked Dwight Widaman, the publisher.

"How about weekly?" he responded. So *Homebodies* was born.

Since then, *Homebodies* has expanded to several other papers and is also distributed as a free online newsletter. The response from readers from Alabama to Alaska is gratifying and enlightening. Through e-mails, phone calls, letters or tapping me on the shoulder in the supermarket, stay-at-home moms share tips and anecdotes for me to pass on to other kindred spirits.

In writing this book I found these ladies to be wonderful resources, and I'm thrilled to include their insights and encouragement in these pages.

I'm also appreciative of the members of the Kansas City Christian Writers' Network, who mentored me as I nurtured this writing career I can perform from home. Many thanks to Cindy Bunch-Hotaling, my editor at InterVarsity Press, for agreeing to listen to "just one more pitch" as she went out the door at the KCCWN writers' conference. Thanks also to Debi Stack and Charlotte Adelsperger, fellow writers who empowered me with their "You go, Girl!" e-mails. And to Bonnie Perry, whose sweet assurance made Christ's presence tangible each time we shared about writing and our families.

Of course I wouldn't have anything to write about if it weren't for my husband, Terry, and our two daughters, Karen and Carrie. Every day is a new adventure in the Gochnauer house. I'm so glad to be planted right in the center of our home and thank Terry for all the extra hours of overtime he's put in and sacrifices he's made so I could be here. I promise we'll buy you another boat someday, Babe.

# 1

........................

# Pick Up Your Cradle
# & Follow Me

I T WAS A MONDAY LIKE ANY OTHER MONDAY, EXCEPT THIS TIME I ARRIVED at work at 8:00 a.m. sharp with a humidifier, three bottles of medicine and a pillow. "I'm okay," I gasped, waving away well-wishers who were maintaining their distance anyway.

Plugging in the humidifier, I hoisted it to the top of the filing cabinet, pushing my daughters' picture aside. A low whirring soon filled the cubicle with moist air for my throbbing throat.

The first of my Type A bosses peeked over the partition. "Great to have you back!" he boomed, dropping another folder in my burgeoning in-box, then disappearing to crank out more.

In no time at all it was 8:15 a.m. and I was exhausted. But I'd missed too many days already and, fever or not, there was work to be done.

By Wednesday my desk was at least back to par. I was even breathing normally, as long as I sat very still. Then the dreaded "Call from Daycare on Line One" blew my business boat out of the water.

Suspicious red spots on my two-year-old, Carrie, were adding panic to another working mom's day. "You'll have to come get her *now,*" the daycare director ordered. Taking as deep a breath as I could . . . cough, hack . . . I wobbled to my supervisor's office.

"What about another babysitter?" he charged.

"They don't want their children exposed to the chicken pox, either."

"Well, can't you get a relative to take care of her?" he persisted.

"All my relatives work."

He was missing the point. My baby was sick and she needed her mommy. That's me. Period.

"Besides, I understand chicken pox only lasts three or four days. I'll be back on Monday." It wasn't as if I didn't have any days coming to me, although I was learning that in a working mom's life the "vacation" days mentioned in my benefits packet actually referred to "sick child" days.

The next Monday was a Monday like any other, except Carrie had new spots. The daycare wouldn't take her. With my own case of chicken fever, I left a message with the receptionist. My normally level-headed boss hit the ceiling, I wore out a box of tissues and my husband, Terry, swore he'd swing things so I could come home with the kids, even if it took us two years to dig out of debt.

"I want you to make up a budget and see what we have to do to get you home." Terry's determined voice calmed me as I dabbed my swollen eyes with a cool cloth.

Encouraged, I dug through our drawers, pulling together receipts, bills and pay stubs. Pretty soon our kitchen table looked a lot like my desk at work, with piles of paper covering its surface. But this time I was working for a different corporation, a private entity comprised of two parents and their children.

### The Stay-at-Home Dream House

The idea of my becoming a stay-at-home mom was not a new one, but it had always seemed beyond our reach. Whenever I'd float the concept to Terry, it was usually in a dreamy context, sort of a wish-upon-a-star kind of conversation. You know . . . those when-the-children-are-asleep-we'll-sit-and-dream talks, where you and your husband discuss what you'd like to be when you grow up.

I wanted to be a stay-at-home mom. Terry wanted our family to be able to eat. The two concepts did not seem to go together, since neither of us was heir to a fortune that would allow us to live on one income. We'd never looked closely at our finances, but since we were barely making it on two paychecks, it was reasonable to assume we'd go under if I quit.

> **We were barely making it with both of us working. We assumed we'd go under if I quit.**

So my dream remained just that, until I was placed in the position of having to choose between the files on my desk and the baby in our crib. Something primal fired inside Terry, and the hesitation he'd felt over shouldering total financial responsibility for his family disappeared.

### Homebodies in the Workforce

Recent statistics reveal that in 71 percent of the married-couple families with children, both parents work (U.S. Department of Labor, May 1998). According to government data, 59 percent of the mothers with children under one year old and 65 percent with children under six were in the labor force. But how many of them really wanted to be there?

Now that workplaces of all types are becoming more accessible and glass ceilings are shattering in record numbers, opportunities for women are booming. This is a positive trend for ambitious females thrilled with the challenge of climbing corporate ladders.

Within the same arena, though, there are strong-minded, capable working mothers who wish they weren't. Believing staying at home is not an option for them, these women are nevertheless committed to making the best of their second-choice situation. They do their jobs well and are valued by their employers as productive members of the team. That's why they're missed when the pesky childcare situation interferes with their work.

### A Calculated Surprise

"This can't be right."

Pulling the calculator closer, I went over the figures again. The result was the same. After subtracting my car payment, daycare for Carrie and her big sister, Karen, taxes and fast-food lunches, I was clearing thirty-nine dollars a week.

It seemed crazy, but it was true. In exchange for less than a dollar an hour, I was sacrificing the dream of raising the girls myself.

Excitedly, I paged Terry at work. "Can you pick up an extra thirty-nine dollars a week in overtime?" I asked.

"Sure!" And with that affirmation I was on my way to becoming a stay-at-home mom. There was a car to be sold and a boss to be told. After that my dream would lie within my grasp.

## The Road Less Traveled

Since I've started down this interesting new path, I've discovered the benefits of becoming a stay-at-home mom stretch across the whole spectrum of family life. There's opportunity for more personal attention to my spouse and children, with the improved chance of truly ministering to those closest to me.

There's the more relaxed pace that has transformed my home into a haven for me and my family. I can set my schedule so I get off work when my husband does, and we can enjoy the evening together without tossing in loads of laundry or vacuuming.

> No longer does a warm forehead signal ominous overtones for more than the ailing child.

There's the excitement of being first on the scene at momentous occasions in my children's lives, instead of finding myself viewing events secondhandedly through a sitter's eyes.

There's the relief of working competently and happily at one job, instead of juggling two full-time careers—one inside the home and one out—and failing to gain satisfaction from either demanding position.

One of the first benefits I appreciated after becoming a stay-at-home mom was the freedom to treat a sick child without going through a committee vote. Which parent will miss work? Whose boss is more understanding? And—I admit this shamefully—if we give her some Tylenol, will her temperature go down and stay down so she can stay in daycare until after my 11:00 a.m. meeting?

These questions are now moot. No longer does a warm forehead in our household signal ominous overtones for more than the ailing child. There's no need for apologetic phone calls to coworkers and department heads after a nervous check of dwindling vacation days, setting my own head pounding in the process.

Instead, I now quietly ease open the bedroom door where my little one snoozes, passed out from a double whammy of antihistamines and decongestants. She sleeps peacefully, knowing Mommy is nearby, armed with backrubs and cool washcloths.

Later, we have a date to color and whisper to Barbies.

Even on sick days I love being a stay-at-home mom.

There are health benefits for mothers, too. How I wish I had been home when I was throwing up every day the first five months of my second pregnancy! Instead, I hugged a public toilet while coworkers shook their heads in sympathy. I got to know the breakroom couch intimately, clutching its scratchy tweed and silently begging for my own mommy during each ten-minute break and lunch hour.

After the baby came, I napped on that same couch during breaks, recuperating from marathon colic sessions the night before. It would have been heavenly to be a stay-at-home mom then, napping when the children napped, and on my own bed. But I didn't know it was an option. I'd never done the math.

### Discovering Your True Wage

In my case, the net gain from my putting in forty hours a week, plus travel time, was only $39. After calculating your own situation, you will most likely arrive at a figure higher or lower. It doesn't matter whether your salary is $15,000 or $50,000 a year. The bottom line is what you're looking for here. After deducting expenses connected with working outside the home every day, how much are you clearing?

Is it worth it?

In chapters three ("Setting Up a Business Plan") and eight ("Life on a Budget"), we'll take a look at some pointers for sorting through bills and paychecks and planning financially for your own proposed jump to home. I don't advocate women quitting their jobs on the spot because their toddler called someone else *Mommy*. When things like that happen to working mothers who wish they could be home anyway, it is devastating. But financial suicide helps no one. We're smart women; let's be smart as we plan our new at-home careers.

If you're a working mother who has already decided you don't want to work full-time anymore but you aren't sure exactly how to accomplish that goal, this is your book. By the time you finish reading it, you will be much closer to your target, and may even discover the final block fitting into that new stay-at-home dream house you're building.

If you're a mom who works and likes it that way, don't misinterpret me as an author seeking to set women's rights back twenty years. This is an empowerment book, not a divisive discourse. A couple should be free to choose whether the mother works outside the home, stays home full-time with her kids, or finds a balance between the two worlds which best fits the family's needs.

> **There's no problem in a woman's asking, "What about me?"**

Perhaps you're wavering, conscious of and thankful for various options but still unsure which choice is right for you. *So You Want to Be a Stay-at-Home Mom* will explore the intricate financial, emotional and spiritual aspects of coming home full-time or part-time, and provide information you need to decide.

### I See That Hand

Many women already intuitively know the pluses of leaving the workplace and concentrating their efforts on the home front. But they've worked hard to get where they are in their careers, and although they may want to put family at the top of their list of priorities, they can have a lot of questions before they make that jump.

Usually books written on being a stay-at-home mom focus on the positive benefits to our children. But there's no problem in a woman also asking, "What about me?" In fact, it's a conscientious mother who checks out all the options before she makes the jump from work to home. Here are some of the issues we'll be examining in *So You Want to Be a Stay-at-Home Mom*:

☐ If I was going to be an at-home mom, why did I go to college?

☐ How do I get my husband's support? What about his mother?

☐ How do I tell my boss and deal with the coworkers I'm leaving behind?

☐ What if I want to resume my career when my children are older?

☐ How can I maintain my business contacts while focusing on my family?

☐ Can my family thrive on a one-income budget?

☐ Are there any special skills I need?

☐ What will I do all day?

☐ How can I use this time at home to encourage my children spiritually?

☐ How can I spark creativity in my children, while nurturing my own personal interests?

☐ Where can I link up with other moms who are also at home?

☐ What can I do to develop confidence as an at-home mom, stay motivated and avoid burnout?

Even if a woman suspects the worst day at home has got to beat the best day at the office, she should be sure to do her homework before she marches up to her boss's desk and resigns. Let no one interpret this book as a call to indiscriminately throw away professional gains in the heat of maternal passions.

Instead a woman should approach her transition to a new, at-home career with the same care and planning she would afford any job change. A solid foundation must be laid. Then if she chooses to become a stay-at-home mom, she can do so confidently and fearlessly, knowing it is the right move for her and her family.

# 2

............................

# Honey,
# You're Home

WHEN A WOMAN DECIDES TO BECOME A STAY-AT-HOME MOM, SHE'S not shirking her responsibility as a productive working member of society. She's simply moving the spot where she does that productive work to inside the home.

So how does her move affect her husband? In my case, Terry was delighted to discover a more relaxed wife, happier children and a house that actually got cleaned. Dinners were homemade more often than not, formerly doomed plants were tended to and lived, and clean underwear was in the drawer when he reached for it.

Scheduling appointments of all kinds became much easier, whether we were meeting with dentists, hairstylists or vets. "When can you come in?" no longer brought a flurry of flipping Daytimer pages as we tried to fit in another obligation.

An increasing number of couples are choosing to let Mom make the transition to becoming a stay-at-home wife. As I spoke with several men whose wives have left full-time employment, I found that no matter what sacrifices had been made, none regretted making that decision. Some were even surprised at how much their families had benefited. Let's take a look at some of their experiences.

### More Time for Fun

Tom, an insurance industry district manager, jokingly says he likes having his wife, Robin, home full-time because he doesn't have to do chores anymore. "It frees up our evenings and weekends for more family time, because we're not doing laundry, running the vacuum and going to the grocery store at night like people do when both parents work.

"The kids seem to be more self-confident and relaxed. They like it because Robin's free to do things at school during the day, like room parenting or having lunch with them, or to go to the pool in the summer."

"Planning a vacation is a lot easier now too," adds Robin, "because you don't have to work around both schedules."

### Exiting Off the Fast Lane

For Glen, who works with the Corps of Engineers, the pressure in the morning getting the kids to daycare is gone. "That was a battle every single day, and the car ride home at night was miserable with the baby crying the whole way home." Although he's had to take on more hours to support the family since his wife, Stacie, came home, Glen appreciates the relief of a less hectic schedule.

### Taking Back the Reins

Dareld, a convenience store assistant manager, says, "The financial side is not easy, and it got tougher when we had another child (born since his wife, Miriam, became an at-home mom). But my children are not being raised by someone else—that was our main motivation in bringing Miriam home."

There are perks, too. "Because I'm off during the week (Monday and Tuesday) and Miriam isn't committed to a full-time job, we are able to go fun places together as a family without running into long lines."

### Parents as Teachers

"Since God gave us the responsibility for Karley," points out Kevin, a

> God honors our decision. That's what makes me feel totally at peace.

machine operator in a Christian publishing house, "we're going to raise her the way he wants us to. Because we're not relying on someone outside the family to watch her, I know exactly what she's being taught all the time.

"Sure, you may not be able to do some of the things or buy some of the things you might like, but we've learned to live within our means. If we have to drive this car longer or live in a less expensive house, it's worth it. I know that God honors our decision. That's what makes me feel totally at peace."

## No More Sick Day Dilemmas

Ben, a warehouse distribution manager, describes the freedom he felt during the two-year period his wife, Rae, stayed home with their three young daughters, Kelsey, Brittni and Alexis, who ranged in age from five to newborn.

"Since I knew Rae was taking care of the girls, I was more available for out-of-town trips that would help me get promoted. I no longer had to juggle my schedule to take the girls to, or pick them up from, daycare." Ben didn't run into the guilt that can accompany overtime, either, because he knew his children were with their mother, not waiting in a childcare center for hours on end.

"When the kids were sick, there wasn't the frantic 'who's gonna take the day off?' or 'are they well enough that you can pump them full of Motrin and send them on their way?' dilemma." Since his girls didn't have to get up at dawn and could nap in their own beds in the afternoons, they were more rested and relaxed, ready to play with Ben when he got home.

## More Patient Parenting

"We had been under heavy debt but were sure Becky needed to be home with our daughters," says Gary, a worship and music pastor. "God answered our prayers by miraculously smoothing out our finances, confirming that he too wanted her home.

"Becky quit work when the girls were entering their elementary-school years. She was more relaxed in the evenings and looked forward to spending time with them instead of coming home from a hard day at work and seeing the kids as another obligation. The patience she had toward them increased, and she wasn't just saying, 'I need my space.'

"After a few years, the kids got older and Becky had more time on her hands to devote to ministry. She started giving piano lessons at home. Many of her students weren't Christians, and she was able to encourage them, reminding them where they got their talent and who they should thank for it."

### Expectant Parents

For Don, a computer consultant, having his wife, Erin, come home after their son was born was something they'd always planned on. "We had the understanding early in our relationship that we would invest like this in our kids. Knowing that ahead of time fostered peace throughout this whole process, and we avoided the tumultuous times we've observed in some marriages.

"We were fortunate to have a lot of friends whose wives had also quit work. Erin and I were both raised with our moms at home, so that was a benefit we've enjoyed ourselves.

"Erin has been able to focus her efforts on our son and really give him a strong educational background. She fostered development in him that we wouldn't have seen in another environment, like daycare. Kurtis isn't even two yet, and he knows his ABCs and numbers. Erin feeds his excitement to learn things. It's neat to see that happen. I don't know that it would have, otherwise. We think it's great having Erin home. It's definitely lived up to our expectations."

> It's great having Erin home. It's definitely lived up to our expectations.

### Financial Faith

Jeff was initially nervous about his wife, Dana, quitting her full-time job to stay home with their daughter, Sammi. "I've got a standard of living I want to keep. It has dropped some; I've stopped buying my toys and spending money where it shouldn't be spent.

"I thought Dana would come home, and then in two or three months, we'd find we couldn't make it and she'd have to go back to work. I've been proven wrong.

"It's funny how God works it out when you say, 'There's no way we're going to be able to make these bills.' Since Dana's come home, I've had tons of overtime available at work. God is providing work when I need to work.

"Dana was always so stressed out over her job. Quitting took tons of pressure off her. With her relaxed, that in turn relaxes me. So we're able to have good communication and not have so many things hanging over our heads."

### A Window in Time
"When we were debating bringing Susan home, she said something that really swayed me more than anything," remembers Ron, a telecommunications specialist. "She said, 'I've got five years before the kids go to school and get focused on other things. That's a one-shot deal, my chance to add my slant to their lives. If I miss that, it's gone.'

"We were always worrying about the kids in daycare, even though we had a very good person taking care of them. They just weren't knowing us like they should. Now we know what they're thinking about, what they're watching and what they're listening to. That's important for our comfort level.

"Susan's a lot happier having the kids under her care, raising them in our family tradition. The girls are going to grow up and make their own decisions, but no matter how they turn out, we'll know we did our best."

### Going with the Flow
The traits of flexibility and respect are crucial in maintaining a healthy marriage, and that's especially true during the time the wife is home. To avoid burnout, neither partner should be nailed into an unbending caricature of a bread-winning macho husband or stay-at-home-if-it-kills-me wife.

As Terry and I have become accustomed to our new lifestyle, we've learned a lot about the shifting weight of responsibility in our marriage, especially on the financial side.

It's been nearly five years since I quit full-time work outside the home. The first year, I was able to be home the entire time, focused completely on getting to know my kids and adjusting to my new routine. We had arranged our expenses in such a way that we were able to get by just fine on Terry's income alone. We adjusted to our revised roles, with me picking up more household chores and Terry working slightly longer hours. We both benefited from my less hectic, more soul-soothing schedule. Our ten-year marriage deepened as we spent more true quality time together.

The second year, God called Terry into a different job, one that paid 30 percent less than the one he had had when I quit work. At first I was frustrated to have to give up my full-time at-home status. But just as I was convinced God had led me home the year before, I also found his hand on me as I searched for a part-time job to make up the difference our family needed. In that wonderful way God has, he gave me a part-time job with limited hours that made up the 30 percent and also allowed me to bring my kids on site with me. (Read about this miraculous time in chapter nine, "God, the Ultimate Money Manager.")

By the third year, Terry was making enough money so I was able to work only one day a week outside the home. When Terry took a nightshift position with his company the fourth year, the increase in pay allowed me to be home full-time again. Because I wasn't working, it didn't matter that Terry was off during the day instead of in the evening; we still got to spend time with each other and with our daughters.

And by the fifth year, God had given me a job I could do at home— writing—that brought in enough money to allow Terry to cut his hours and get back on the day shift.

By trying to be flexible and open to whatever comes our way, Terry and I—as well as the other families who have shared their thoughts in this chapter—are able to avoid, or at least minimize, barriers that hinder us from spending lots of time raising and encouraging our children.

"I want my boys to say, 'Our parents had time for us,'" says Dwayne,

> **It isn't your culture, your race or your gender. It's not how much money or potential you have in life.**

whose wife, Julie, is at home raising their two sons, Levi and Marshall. "No matter how rich you are, you cannot extend that twenty-four-hour day.

"My friends may say, 'Having your wife home might work in a perfect world.' But it's only perfect because Julie and I work at it every day. It isn't your culture, your race or your gender. It's not how much money or potential you have in life. It's the priorities we've set for our family.

"Julie and I are actually happier, more financially secure and better able to control the money we do have since we only have one income to account for. People can't believe that would be true, but it is, if you do things right and take the time to make it work."

If you're a husband who's been skeptical about this stay-at-home mom idea, take heart. Read on, and join your wife in examining steps you can take as a couple in exploring the at-home option. Many have gone before you; more families are making this choice every day. If you so choose, you also have the opportunity to change the tempo of your family life, the chance to take the ramp off the fast lane.

# 3

......................

# Setting Up Your Family Business Plan

**Y**OUR FAMILY—THE ULTIMATE SMALL BUSINESS—CAN ONLY BENEFIT when you and your husband take the time to examine specific reasons for bringing you home, while planning how to make that transition as smooth as possible.

To aid you as you consider all the ins and outs of making this change, I suggest you draw up a personal family business plan. The term *business plan* sounds rather officious, but it doesn't have to be complicated. Setting down a general outline of goals and objectives allows families to take charge of their proposed lifestyle change. It also minimizes the chance of being broadsided by some aspect they hadn't considered.

You might check out the resource section of your local library and take a look at books, magazines and newspaper articles which relate to drawing up plans for small businesses. After studying these examples, pull out the best parts of each to frame your own plan for your family.

At the end of this chapter you will see a sample family business plan.

Take a look at it, and then continue reading the chapter to see how I use this sample plan to help keep myself focused. Keep in mind that this is just an example. Talk through each section carefully with your spouse, adding or subtracting items that relate specifically to your own family. Your mate may have expectations that are different from yours. Cooperate and compromise to find common ground, forging a personalized plan together.

## Purpose

"To create a secure and happy home where my children can flourish spiritually, physically, mentally and socially as I love, teach and encourage them. I'll give them the top spot in my list of priorities, right after cultivating my relationships with God and my husband." As time goes on and challenges arise, I'll have this mission statement to go back to.

What do Terry and I generally hope to accomplish? By allowing me to spend an average of fifty more hours a week with our children than I did when I was working full-time, we are giving the girls a better look at their parents walking with Christ in everyday life. Within our marriage, we want to reduce the stress level brought on by serving too many masters at the same time. And now that I'm here to clean it, our house looks better than it has in years.

## Roles

Terry is primary breadwinner, spiritual leader and tickle monster of our family. His children are precious to him. Since we can't both be home full-time, Terry is determined to do what he can to allow me to be there as much as possible. He's gratified to know that by working a few hours more a week he's facilitating an emotional renewal throughout our family and strengthening his marriage and his children.

As my mission statement says, my primary focus is nurturing the spiritual, physical, mental and social well-being of our children. Terry's focus is the same; we've just decided that I'm the one who gets to spend the most "hands-on" time with Karen and Carrie.

My secondary job is to stretch Terry's paycheck to cover our expenses and to be willing to work part-time, if necessary, to get us over occasional financial humps that can't be flattened out by cutting costs. We have amicably divided household chores. I don't ask Terry to do as much around the house as he did when I worked full-time, but by mutual agreement he is still responsible for some tasks.

> Christ is the leader of our management team.

Our carefully laid plan falls apart without God's influence.. So Christ is the leader of our management team, providing guidance through his Holy Spirit. We access this guidance through reading the Bible, remembering the importance of daily prayer and regular fellowship with other Christians. We also watch expectantly for answers to our prayers. His affirmations have buoyed us through many tough times that could easily have swamped us.

### Children

Specific traits we want to cultivate in Karen and Carrie are *confidence* through the knowledge that their parents and God will love and guide them; *compassion* as they learn to interact peaceably with others and *leadership* as they gain important skills they need to succeed both personally and professionally. We also want to build *strong moral character* in them so they will live their lives according to the plans God has for them, "plans to give [them] hope and a future" (Jeremiah 29:11).

What did the kids think about my coming home? The first two months after I quit work, my two-year-old followed me from room to room, as if she didn't want to let me out of her sight. (I understand this is a common phenomenon when Mom initially comes home.) Karen, who was a first-grader at the time, loved coming straight home after school instead of going into daycare for several hours each afternoon. My girls each gave me two thumbs up for my decision.

It's not just little kids who appreciate having mom around more. I found the following comment from a teen in *Parade* magazine, July 26, 1998.

"Recently, my mom switched from full-time to part-time work, so she could be home when my sister and I got home from school. Because of this, our family came together, whereas before we were falling apart. Now that my mom's home, we can talk to each other and things around the house get done. . . . When my mom was working, I had learned to be self-sufficient, but it got to the point that it was too much" (Shauna N., 17, Oklahoma City, Oklahoma).

## Budget

As I mentioned in chapter one, I gathered all my financial papers—pay stubs, checkbook, savings-account records, installment-loan payment books, utility bills. I took out a legal pad and drew twelve columns, one for each month of the previous year. Then I listed all our expenses, everything right down to the cash we kept out of every check for "spending money." For each category (i.e., housing, groceries, installment loans, etc.), I took the twelve-month total and divided it to come up with an average monthly amount.

Patterns started emerging. For instance, I noticed I tend to binge in the grocery store around the Fourth of July and Christmas. I hadn't realized that until I saw it on paper, and now I'm more cautious about watching my food dollars around the holidays.

I used the same formula to come up with a monthly average on all the other categories too. By lining everything out, I could see potential budget busters, like the yearly property taxes and quarterly insurance premiums. Money would need to be set aside in a savings account each month so these periodic bills could be paid when they came due.

As you look at the sample budget outline at the end of this chapter, you'll want to insert and revise categories to reflect your own family's particular expenses. Are you paying tuition for private school? How about regular charges for pharmaceuticals or medical treatments? Perhaps you have a standing Friday-night date with your spouse and pay a teen to watch the kids a few hours each week while you go out. Note every expenditure you can think of, large or small.

Make sure you have made provisions for life and health insurance coverage, either by transferring everyone in the family to your husband's policy or by purchasing affordable private insurance.

Also if your family is considering refinancing your home or purchasing a big-ticket item, be sure to do that before Mom quits. Avoid getting hurt by the catch-22 of wanting to cut monthly costs through refinancing but no longer being able to qualify for the loan because your husband's salary alone isn't enough to satisfy a banker.

After you get everything tallied and compare your income (salary, dividends or monies from other sources) with your expenses, you will probably discover some things are going to have to go to enable your family to make it with just one of you working.

In our case, deleting a car payment helped bring fixed monthly expenses under control. Getting rid of that costly obligation, along with childcare expenses, went a long way toward clearing the way for me to come home. Terry's truck was already paid off, and we replaced my vehicle with a dependable car we could purchase with cash.

As my husband and I continued streamlining our expenses, we found we were able to get the day-to-day bills honed but were still immobilized by huge credit card debt left over from a failed business. I despaired as I considered the massive balance standing between my being with my kids and interest charges that ate up most of the ground gained with each monthly payment.

Then I went out to lunch with a girlfriend who reminded me of my rich 401(k) account. We would take a tremendous hit—state and federal taxes and penalties would eat up almost 50 percent of the amount we withdrew—but when the dust cleared, there would be enough left over to cancel our debt.

Yes, it would mean tapping into our retirement funds. But we believed our commitment to our children now was more important than our commitment to ourselves several decades in the future. Plus we still had plenty of time to rebuild our nest egg.

Terry and I took our lumps and paid off that credit card balance, and the door to my coming home swung open.

Will the same move work for your family? Talk to a financial planner, carefully examining the pros and cons of your individual situation before you act. You and your husband will have to decide what items—whether they be cars, savings plans, hobbies or styles of housing—are expendable and which are not.

Bringing freewheeling spending into line lays the crucial cornerstone in this stay-at-home dream house you're building. Without cutting costs and curbing the appetite for material things, there is no way this house can stand for the long haul. It may take a bit longer than you would like to get your family in a secure monetary position, but don't let yourself get discouraged. Take heart—the eventual payoff is worth the wait.

As far as practicing living on one income, Terry and I were confident we could make it on his salary alone from the moment the figures jibed on the note pad. Remember, when I did the math and projected the necessary cuts, I realized we were very close—within forty dollars a week—of being able to live on what Terry normally brought home. It didn't take very long at all for us to feel comfortable with the idea of giving up my paycheck.

In actuality, two months passed between the afternoon when the "GO" light flashed green and the day our new budget allowed me to walk out the door. The luxury car finally sold, and we paid off our credit card balance. I had also taken steps to ensure I didn't leave my employer stranded, which was important since I didn't know if I'd want to hire back on later.

Depending upon their comfort level, a couple may practice living on one income for several weeks, several months, a year or longer. Go with the time schedule that best fits your personal situation.

**Maintaining Skills**
Since I already had a computer at home and much of my work at the office had been done on a computer, I continued to track the latest software trends. When I realized I wanted to pursue a different career, writing, instead of going back into the office work I had done before, I began attending local writers' group meetings and read every book on journalism and creative writing I could get my hands on. I participated in writers' retreats, workshops and conferences and continue to strengthen my skills in this way.

In chapter five ("Resuming Your Career Once the Kids Are Older"), various suggestions are listed on maintaining business contacts and keeping yourself sharp for reentering the workforce at a later date. Your personal business plan should specifically note people you will stay in touch with, classes you will take to enhance your skills and memberships and licenses you will keep up to date.

### Long-Range Goals

When we originally made our plan, Terry and I left open the door to my returning to full-time work. We did, however, decide that it would not be before our younger child started kindergarten.

Part-time work was penciled in as a possibility, depending on our financial situation at the time. It turned out that when I did need to take a part-time job, it was during school hours (Karen was in class) and I negotiated placing Carrie, who was a preschooler, at the on-site daycare at no charge. My time away from the girls was minimized.

Now that you've examined the detailed points of a simple family business plan, you can better determine specific areas that need attention before Mom resigns. Instead of leaping into turbulent waters with your eyes shut, you and your spouse can enjoy the refreshing renewal of a well-thought-out transformation.

> **Enjoy the refreshing renewal of a well-thought-out transformation.**

As I write this, Karen and Carrie are both elementary students. Now that I have been home for several years, I can see myself continuing in the same vein indefinitely. In fact, I wonder sometimes whether my daughters need me more now than they did before. Whenever I say something like "When I go back to work," both girls shout, "No, Mommy!" and jump on me.

Guess they want my undivided attention a bit longer.

\*    \*    \*    \*

**Sample Family Business Plan Outline**

I. Purpose

    A. Mission statement (see chapter seventeen, "Developing a Personal Mission Statement")

    B. What in general do we hope to accomplish in bringing Mom home?

II. Management team roles—where do we each fit?

    A. Dad

    B. Mom

    C. God

III. Children

    A. What specific traits do we want to cultivate in our children?

    B. How will Mom's expanded presence at home lend itself to building these traits in them?

    C. What do the kids think about Mom coming home?

IV. Budget

    A. Income

        1. Wages

        2. Interest/dividends

        3. Benefits paid by husband's company

            a. medical/dental

            b. life insurance

            c. retirement plans

        4. Rental income

        5. Other

    B. Expenses

        1. Tithe

        2. Housing

        3. Utilities

        4. Insurance

        5. Savings

        6. Taxes

        7. Installment loans

        8. Credit cards

        9. Maintenance and repairs

  10. Groceries/household items/toiletries

  11. Dining out/entertainment

  12. Department stores

  13. Medical

  14. Pets

  15. Children's sports and recreation

  16. Other

 C. What are we willing to give up in order to bring our expenses in line with our reduced income? What are we not willing to give up?

 D. How long will we practice living on one income before Mom turns in her resignation?

V. Maintaining skills

 A. Will Mom maintain some of her present business contacts? If so, name them.

 B. What will she do to develop new skills for a possible future change of vocation?

 C. Will Mom take any classes while she is home?

 D. What seminars and retreats will she attend?

 E. Where will the children be while she is in training?

 F. Will she continue her current memberships in professional organizations? What new groups will she join?

 G. Do any of her professional licenses or certificates need to be renewed periodically?

VI. Long-range goals

 A. How long will Mom stay home?

 B. Is Dad able to work overtime?

 C. Will Mom work part time? If so, will she work inside or outside the home? What is the maximum amount of hours she will work? Where will the children be while she is working?

 D. Decide on a future date when you will review your family business plan and see if you're accomplishing your goals.

# 4

·····················

# Will My
# Professional
# Training Go
# to Waste?

**I**F THERE WAS EVER SOMEONE WHO WOULD BE VOTED "MOST LIKELY TO rabidly pursue a career," I was that person. I was one of those gung-ho 1970s graduates who vigorously flung their tasseled caps in the air, chanting "I am woman; hear me *roar*!" and raced out to meet the world.

Doors of opportunity were springing open. Glass ceilings were shattering. I was determined to leave the kitchen sink and everything connected to it behind.

An undernourished bank account posed a major roadblock on my path to success, but I was on a mission to obtain my degree. Through sheer strength of will I managed to cram four years of college into seven. I bartered my overachiever grade point for a few small scholarships that put a dent in tuition fees. I worked a couple of semesters ("Hi! Welcome to Wendy's! May I take your order?") and went to school a couple of semesters. I took out student loans.

One bright May morning, I finally hung a college diploma on my wall, redirected my quest and marched on toward the bright business world.

## Right Attitude, Wrong Road

What does this have to do with you? Well, my point is this: We each want to succeed and have worked hard to do so. It may have been through struggling to grasp an advanced degree or putting in long hours straight out of high school to achieve excellence in your field. I know what it feels like to go after a career prize wholeheartedly, to pursue it with purpose and determination, yet slowly realize the brass ring hangs from a tree growing on a completely different course.

> It's the infamous Mommy Track, in the absolute best sense of the term.

For me, that alternate course runs through a playground where my children swing. There, peanut butter and jelly sandwiches on our bellies in the grass beat out croissants with a client any day. It's the infamous Mommy Track, in the absolute best sense of the term. Not a sidetrack where a woman is destined to languish, buried in a pile of diapers and laundry, but a wonderful stroll down a quieter lane far removed from the fast track of Corporate America. Or, at least, as far removed as she would choose to be.

I'm sure the imagined prospect of throwing away their college degree and work experience preys heavily on many working moms weighing the idea of coming home. But no one can take your education or experience away from you, and that knowledge can be a wonderful asset as you tackle your new position as a stay-at-home mom.

Once you and your husband have determined important personal and family goals, you can use your background to further those objectives.

## Let's Get Real

Rather than talk in abstracts, let's take a look at some real-world examples from my own college transcript. After considering these pictures from my personal album, you'll want to take a close look at your unique training to see how classes you've taken and experience you've gained plug into your plans on the home front.

As I scan my educational record, each course springs from the page, asserting its applicability to family life. These business classes have served me many times over. Insights on insurance planning and cost-comparison budgeting both grew out of knowledge gained in Personal Finance 101. Whether preparing our yearly income taxes, balancing the checkbook, or saving for retirement, the techniques I learned in these courses have come in handy.

Then there are the lessons I received in civics and government. My children have benefited from my political science classes practically since birth. The first time my daughter, Karen, saw a voter's registration card, she was four months old. Her eyes followed the white card curiously as I explained the power of one vote.

Lifting her up to see the multipaged ballot and shiny puncher, I coached her. "Your vote counts just as much as the mayor's. As soon as you're old enough, you should make your voice heard. Don't just sit idly and let others determine the fate of your city and country. This is important!"

Karen smiled a toothless grin, then spit up on my shoulder.

I'm sure others have had the same impulse Karen did while standing in the voting booth, but at least I've been able to teach her and her little sister in the years since then to value the opportunity to go to the polls when they come of age.

Sociology classes mapped cultural interaction between races and explored various elements of our multifaceted society. Expanding on that teaching, I encourage my daughters to value all levels of human life, from the weakest to the most affluent.

As children learn to appreciate other people's needs, they can join their parents in charitable work. Whether through a local church or a community outreach center, kids have the opportunity to help serve dinners at homeless shelters, give part of their allowance as an offering or donation to support missionaries throughout the world, or sort through gently-used clothing and toys to pass on to less fortunate children. Teens can get involved by tutoring younger students at school and by helping renovate homes for low-income families.

I would say the most beneficial training I received prior to becoming a stay-at-home mom came from my various interpersonal communication classes. Implementing conflict resolution techniques, adapting a message for a specific audience, improving listening skills—I use these lessons on a daily basis as I raise my preschooler, counsel my preteen and maintain a solid marriage with their father.

Okay, so maybe the anthropology course is a throwaway. Or is it? At the very least I'm armed when my elementary student comes home from public school filled with questions about the origin of the human race. As I point her toward the Creator, I am able to counter humanist views because I debated those same teachings in college.

### Do Try This at Home

No matter what form your higher education took, there's a good chance you can use the principles you learned at home.

"I feel the college experience enhances motherhood," says Debi, a former magazine editor who now works as a home-based writer while raising two young children. "You learn to set primary and subsidiary goals, juggle tasks simultaneously, meet deadlines and deal with all kinds of personalities."

Shauna, an expecting wife and mother of a toddler, struggled with leaving her job, but devotion to her children outweighed her love of her students. "I spent a long time studying to be a French teacher, even living in France and going to school there. This year will be my tenure year, and I'm giving it up. I don't know if I'll be back.

"I am of the opinion that the choice wouldn't be so hard if society made it easier to be a part-time professional," she continues. "I don't have any control over the society issue, so I had to make the decision based on what I wanted with my family. I can tell you that there is a difference between my students whose moms are around and those that aren't. As a teacher who

> The choice wouldn't be so hard if society made it easier to be a part-time professional.

sees the results of this, I just couldn't go on being away from my son."
Shauna is now considering giving private French lessons in her home.
Because she left her school on good terms, her chances of linking up with
and providing additional tutoring for former and new students is excellent.

There's no one stereotype to fit the multi-talented women who choose
to put their gifts to work at home. Cheryl uses her piano background to
nurture her children's musical talents; Jennifer's English degree comes in
handy as she volunteers at her son's school library and helps check his
written essays. Erin, a former physical therapist, works on her two-year-
old's proprioception (balance) skills as he scrambles over his turtle sand-
box.

Rae employs her sales and customer-services skills to obtain the best
deals for her family, whether out in public or on her home turf. Dana draws
on her counseling background as she communicates with her toddler,
builds a strong marriage with her husband and works at her computer as
her child naps, developing a support group for infertile couples.

Susan's accounting background helps her keep her family's finances
balanced and in the black. Martha's elementary education degree made
homeschooling her two kids a natural choice. Miriam challenges her
children to expand their view of other nations, spurred by her own
experience as a missionary kid and the training she received in her position
with her denomination's world headquarters.

### It Was Not for Naught

Whether you eventually return to work outside the home or not, your trip
to college and/or work experience was certainly not wasted, and the
knowledge you accumulated there doesn't have to lay dormant as you take
a more active role in raising your children.

Are you a history major? Explore family genealogy and take field trips
with your children to famous sites, especially ones where a relative might
have played a role. For instance, about an hour's drive away from our home
is a cemetery where my daughters' two great-great-great-uncles are buried.
These brothers fought on opposite sides in the Civil War (one as a private,
the other as a brigadier general). Touring the graves and surrounding

battleground sites allows us to discuss not only the cataclysmic war that ripped America a century ago but also how societal issues can divide families. Illuminate current events in light of past history, especially noting God's sovereignty revealed throughout the ages.

Do you have a science background? Help children formulate age-appropriate experiments at home, carefully computing data and expanding their cognitive learning. Get outside and introduce them to unusual plants and animals native to your area, pointing out God's amazing use of diversity in the world. Intrigue youngsters through challenging projects, and encourage them to enter their creations in competitions and science fairs.

Are you a computer whiz? You'll be a pro at maintaining your own CPU at home, updating equipment and tracking industry trends. Take the kids on personalized tours of the Internet and World Wide Web, downloading freeware and shareware games and educational programs. Organizing family records and finances will be a snap. You can probably even generate some extra income by working part-time from home, if you so choose, repairing or updating friends' computers and helping new users learn their way around the Internet.

> Their stay-at-home mom is the most important teacher her children will ever encounter.

For obvious reasons an education degree fits perfectly into the life of a stay-at-home mom, who is the most important teacher her children will ever encounter. You might even try homeschooling, taking advantage of a new flexible schedule that allows more time for field trips and personal instruction.

Think about the position you now hold as you consider changing your profession from one focused outside to one centered inside the home. How can the insights, skills and knowledge you have gained from your area of study be carried over to your family? The answers are as individual as each reader. But you might be surprised to discover how much of what you now do for others can directly benefit your family and community when you make the jump to home.

## Take Another Look

Here are a few more hints on using your present job skills at home. What ideas do they give you for better utilizing your own abilities at home and in volunteer capacities?

*Secretary:* Scheduling appointments and school activities (no small feat in a busy family), dealing with solicitors, handling correspondence, organizing papers and using computer skills to streamline household records. Volunteer opportunities: The PTA, your kids' scouting program, a worthy not-for-profit organization or your church would love a share of your expertise!

*Interior decorator:* Designing a warm and inviting home, from painting and wall-papering to sewing curtains and furniture coverings. Choosing the right color and texture the *first* time, stretching the family's decorating budget. Volunteer opportunities: Women's groups like MOPS (see appendix A: "Resources for Mom") would welcome you as a speaker or demonstrator.

*Personnel manager:* Assigning children ability-appropriate duties; implementing conflict-resolution skills to deal with sibling rivalry and communication problems; recognizing specific talents in your children and then nourishing those gifts. Volunteer opportunities: Use your skills to help church workers find their niche.

*Accountant:* One-income budgeting; tax preparation; using coupons and comparison shopping; financial and retirement planning. Volunteer opportunities: Of course your child's PTA could use your expertise, but don't forget your church or charitable organization. Many ministry leaders are great with people but lacking in financial skills and would welcome your guidance when the time comes to put together next year's budget.

*Teacher:* Preschool instruction; homework monitor; confident interaction with school authorities. Volunteer opportunities: You have the perfect background to become the best club leader, Sunday-school teacher or room mother your child ever had!

*Chef:* Menu planning; drawing on nutritional expertise while preparing healthy foods for your family; developing feasts for special occasions, using economical but tasty substitutions while preparing entrees at the lowest cost possible. Volunteer opportunities: Offer your special gift to your church and they will eat it up!

*Nurse:* Ensuring family members get regular checkups; monitoring growth progress; always available for her own children when they are sick, hurt or needing that special attention only Mom can give. Volunteer opportunities: Signing on as nurse at your children's camp can be a wonderful experience for you and your kids.

*Researcher:* Encouraging kids to learn about their heritage; keeping up scrapbooks and mementos; telling stories about their ancestors and living relatives; taking pictures and starting diaries. Volunteer opportunities: You have abundant ministry potential. Offer to become your church's historian. Or consider helping teen mothers capture their positive experiences in a baby book, helping senior adults record their life stories or helping hospice patients record a legacy for their families.

*Assembly-line worker:* Organizing various household tasks for efficiency; keeping an eye on accomplishing daily goals; emphasizing the importance of an individual's contribution in the overall scheme of things. Volunteer opportunities: Your child's teacher would welcome your help on the time-consuming tasks that transform a classroom from good to great.

*Childcare provider:* Meeting the physical and mental needs of your own young children through play and insightful instruction; creating fun activities to challenge and entertain. Volunteer opportunities: What a difference you could make in the life of a teen mother who needs a mentor!

So you see, there are plenty of ways to turn your college degree and job experience into useful tools that will benefit you at home and in your community. But even if you can't figure out a single way to use your particular degree, don't let that stop you from becoming a stay-at-home mom, if that's where your heart is. Your kids don't care what you studied, as long as you study them more.

# 5

..........................

# Resuming Your Career Once the Kids Are Older

W ELL-ESTABLISHED RESEARCH LAUDS THE FIRST FIVE YEARS OF LIFE as crucial, formative years. Since no one else can provide Mom's unique insight and direction, many formerly content career women find themselves plunged into a confusing quandary once they become parents. Who takes priority—the child or the job? And whichever way she chooses, how does a woman handle the resulting sense of loss?

Ecclesiastes 3 describes "a time for everything, and a season for every activity under heaven." In the spirit of that passage I'd like to say there's a time to focus on work and a time to focus on raising children. Matthew 6:24 mentions the hazards of trying to serve two masters: "Either he will hate the one and love the other, or he will be devoted to the one and despise the other."

For me it boiled down to flipflopping my priorities. Instead of giving my employer the lion's share of my day, I could give my children the choice part. I haven't forgotten my plans for a productive career, but now those goals simmer as I turn my attention to the more important work at hand—building a solid foundation in the lives of my children.

When a woman chooses to become a stay-at-home mom, it's not necessarily a lifelong decision. In many families Mom plans to re-enter the business world after her children reach school age. She may worry, however, that she'll have problems breaking back into her profession once she's ready to do so.

This is a valid concern, and if you're planning to go back to work when the kids get older, there are some definite steps you should consider while you're at home.

> **If you're planning to go back to work later, there are definite steps you should consider now.**

### "Goodbye" or "See You Later"?

First of all, do you want to go back to the same company, or even the same line of work?

During my first year as a stay-at-home mom, my daughters were six and two, and I felt that I had a lot of catching up to do with each of them. I still valued my friends and associates at work, however.

So I kept in contact with several people at my former company, making phone calls every few weeks and scheduling lunch dates while my kids visited with their own peers. In this manner I was able to keep abreast of the ebb and flow of this familiar workplace, as well as maintain friendships with my former coworkers.

If there is any possibility you will want to return to the same company where you presently work, schedule a formal meeting with your supervisors to make them aware of your plans before you leave.

New employee training expenses can be astronomical, and rehiring a capable former worker benefits companies with an eye on the bottom line. In discussing your future plans with your bosses, you may find they have some suggestions for keeping your foot in the door. This is especially true when you are viewed as a valued employee, a perception you will only intensify as you take a professional approach to leaving your job.

As most companies increase their dependence on computers, you may be able to freelance from your home via personal computer and modem—your own or your employer's. Don't overlook the possibility of working part-time in your home office even a few hours a week while your children nap.

After you become a stay-at-home mom, be sure to take advantage of opportunities to attend any informal functions (such as retirement and promotion parties) where you'll see your former supervisors. Let them see that just because you're at home, you're not dead! Show them the new sparkle in your well-rested eyes, and be prepared when someone asks you how it's going. Instead of focusing specifically on the kids' latest escapades, talk about the renewal you feel as a full-time parent and the way shaping another individual's future has changed your life.

Healthy self-esteem is very attractive in an employer's eyes. Your supervisor will regret ever letting you get away.

### Top Ten List for Improving Your Chances of Being Rehired

**1.** Occasionally call or visit work friends and associates.

**2.** Keep abreast of company changes and the evolution of different departments, especially your former department and those departments you might be interested in working with in the future. Contact the personnel office periodically and check on job postings, which will give you some insight as to new positions being created and areas of growth within the company.

**3.** Ask to remain on the mailing list for the office newsletter, and keep up on employee achievements. Send congratulatory notes to supervisors and coworkers celebrating special business successes such as promotions and employment anniversaries. Congratulate them on personal milestones, too, such as engagements or new babies.

**4.** Update professional licenses and certificates, even if you're not using them right now. Don't allow them to lapse if you intend to put them to use in the future. It's much smarter to maintain your present level of certification than to allow yourself to backslide, making catching up later more difficult.

5. Sign up for an occasional evening or weekend course at the local college, or undergo periodic testing to renew and sharpen skills. Take the opportunity to enroll in classes that will improve your chances for promotion if you choose to return to the workplace.

6. Continue memberships in professional organizations, and don't miss a meeting. When you attend such functions, dress in business attire.

7. Attend cutting-edge conferences and retreats whenever possible. Once again, dress appropriately—skip the jeans and sundresses, even if everyone else is wearing them. Outfit yourself just a little bit more formally than the others; aim to look polished instead of ostentatious.

8. Read current periodicals and books, keeping your finger on the pulse of your profession. Watch the news, both local and national.

9. If you have access to the Internet, use it to find the most up-to-the-minute information on your former company and its competitors. Read newsgroup postings and participate in international chatroom discussions with people in your field. The next time you run into your supervisors, surprise them with your knowledge of industry trends.

10. Usually the world will view you as you view yourself. Set the tone—project the air of a competent professional, whether working at home or in the office, and others will respond to you in the same manner.

### I'm Outta Here

If you have made the jump to home from a position you weren't especially fond of anyway, you now have the chance to redirect your working life—or recognize God's redirecting it for you.

The hectic schedule of a working mom challenges the most organized woman, as each day begins like a blast out of a chute—rush to daycare, rush to work, rush to do errands at lunch, rush back to work, rush to daycare, rush to the grocery, rush home, rush supper, rush house cleaning, rush the kids to bed so she can have a moment's peace, rush to the pillow to rush in six hours of sleep before she starts this all over again the next day.

Granted, there will be times when as a stay-at-home mom you'll find yourself experiencing a day just as maddening as the one outlined above.

> With a more relaxed schedule, you'll have time to figure out what you want to do with your life.

But the sheer number of pressure-cooker experiences drops once you've removed yourself from the constant rush-hour madness. No more raising children from the dead every morning by the glow of the Snoopy night-light and then threatening them as they reject a breakfast they're not hungry for yet. No more bundling babies up like mummies and charging to the sitter's before daybreak.

You'll see the difference in your children, and you'll feel the difference in yourself, as life begins to wind down a bit. And with the more relaxed schedule you'll discover you actually have time to figure out what you want to do with your life, beyond the precious commitment you have already made to your husband and your children.

## A Time for Writing

I'm a writer. I love being a writer. Just a few years back I didn't have a clue that I would enjoy writing or be successful at it. It wasn't until I was home with my children that I realized there was another professional route I should be taking instead of the road that had brought me this far.

I believed God had affirmed my husband's and my decision for me to stay at home with Carrie and Karen. That meant he would provide for all our needs according to his riches, especially when, as is often true on the budget of a one-income family, we didn't have any riches of our own.

> He will provide for all our needs according to his riches.

One winter, God revealed himself so clearly in providing for our finances, it was absolutely undeniably his doing. Mouths dropped open all over our church. But none gaped open farther than our own. A friend suggested, "You should write this down!" So I did.

Terry watched the girls one Saturday while I sat at my ancient, green-screened computer and pounded out "God, the

Ultimate Money Manager," my testament to God's faithfulness in acknowledging our new commitment to tithing. Soon I was passing out copies at church, ensuring that none of our praying friends would forget what God had done for our family.

Little did I know that one of the women who attended our church was the managing editor of a book publishing house. A copy of my testimony providentially arrived in her hands. She tapped the shoulder of an editor she knew, and before the year was out, my family's picture was on the cover of our denominational magazine, with my article running as the feature story. (You can find "God, the Ultimate Money Manager" in chapter nine.)

Not only did the story bless readers, it opened my eyes to a new career path for me. And it was one that could be traveled at home without compromising my commitment to my young children.

I love my new career. Here's a straightforward plan for making your own career change.

### Top Ten List for Planning a Future Career

1. Make sure it's something you'll really enjoy. Take time to carefully think through your personal and professional goals, and choose a new direction that will give you more satisfaction than you formerly experienced in the workplace.

2. Garner your husband's support. Whether you develop a new career that will take you back into the workplace after the kids are in school (or some other milestone you have tentatively set) or you strike upon a job you can perform from home, be sure your mate is rooting for you.

3. The date of your anticipated return to work should be completely flexible. Don't plant a time bomb that stresses out you or your family.

4. If you already know someone who is in your dream job, ask if you can interview the person, thereby gathering invaluable insight as to the inner-workings of your proposed profession. Develop a positive relationship with your contact through occasional letters, phone calls and lunches.

5. Pinpoint local companies as prospective future employers. Use the Internet and print media to gather information on these companies and their competitors; keep abreast of industry changes and how these changes

affect local employers.

**6.** Develop and polish skills by signing up for evening or weekend courses at a local college, or tackle correspondence courses you can study at home.

**7.** Join professional organizations and attend their meetings, especially when workshops are given. Training and networking gleaned through such classes are invaluable in building skills and confidence.

**8.** Plan to acquire any necessary licenses or certificates, as appropriate.

**9.** If possible, do some freelancing from home in your new field—even if you aren't paid a lot—to test yourself. Early in my writing career I began writing an unpaid column for other stay-at-home moms for my local newspaper. The experience I gained in developing my writing skills and meeting weekly deadlines proved priceless.

**10.** "Unless the LORD builds the house, its builders labor in vain" (Psalm 127:1). This is true of your present plans to become a fulfilled and happy stay-at-home mom, as well as in considering your future career outside the home. Don't make a move in either direction without God's clear leading.

The same God who provided a new and exciting professional direction in my life is willing to work in your life, too. What makes this so thrilling is that God knows us right down to our toes—even better than we know ourselves—and he has the benefit of knowing what the future holds for us. With what better person could we entrust our professional and personal goals?

# 6
.......................

# How Do I
# Tell My Boss?

**N**O ONE COULD TELL A JOKE OR MOTIVATE ME TO MEET A DEADLINE quite like George. George was the best boss I ever had, even if he did lose it that hectic morning when I chose Carrie and her chicken pox over him and his charts and graphs. If he hadn't gotten so upset, I never would have been pushed to search for the key that opened the door to my coming home.

Gee, George—thanks!

He pouted for a week after I told him I was leaving. Since we were friends as well as coworkers, I finally asked for a few minutes of his time behind closed doors. Basically, I asked him as respectfully as I could to *snap out of it!*

Now I don't suggest you do the same thing with your own boss. George and I had worked together for four years and had shared many open conversations about God and an individual's purpose in his plan—even as we were climbing mountains of company paperwork. Once he got past how my leaving would temporarily affect his department's timetables, George realized I was finally acting on those deeply-held convictions we had already discussed.

Several years have passed since I waved goodbye to my job, with many of my colleagues taking bets on how soon I'd be back. George has retired himself, but we still keep in regular contact through luncheon dates and the ease of e-mail.

I would guess George understands better than most people the renaissance I've gone through since I reprioritized my life. What a freedom there is in deciding upon one full-time job and then doing that one job well! No more struggling through each day with no time to think about tomorrow. No more turning around and realizing another year is gone, then another.

My daughter Karen's first six years are gone. No use crying over it, but there's no use in shuffling her next six into a secondary position on my to-do list either. If you feel the same way, and you and your spouse have found the path to bring you home without endangering your family financially or emotionally, then you've got to take the next step: You've got to tell your boss.

## Plan Your Exit Carefully

But as you prepare to share your decision, be sure you are ready. No matter how unhappy you may be in your position, don't storm in, toss your keys on your supervisor's desk and slam the door behind you. This scenario may look great in the movies, but it doesn't play well in real life. You're a professional; be a professional until you walk out the door, whether there's a going-away party or not.

If you want to do this right, you need to make sure you've reinforced any potential weak spots in your plan. Then you can have that liberating talk with your supervisor.

Depending on your circumstances, anywhere from two weeks to six months or longer may pass between the time you decide to come home and the day you actually head out to the employee parking lot for the last time.

Don't pull back on production and glide toward your resignation date. Instead, concentrate on leaving your boss with the very best memories of your work habits. After all, you may be asking for your job back or asking for a reference in a few years. Shortsightedness could hinder your future prospects.

So how does an exemplary employee say goodbye? Here are some to-dos for your list.

### Before You Resign

☐ Know exactly why you're leaving, and be committed to that reason. If you keep swaying back and forth between "should I or shouldn't I?" you shouldn't.

☐ Be like-minded with your husband. The new lifestyle you're planning will demand sacrifices from both of you. Make sure he shares the desire to have you home with the children on Your full-time basis.

> Concentrate on leaving your boss with the very best memories of your work habits.

☐ Formulate a personalized family business plan. (Check chapter three, "Setting Up Your Family Business Plan.")

☐ Bring finances in line, and then practice living on one income for a period of time—perhaps three to six months. By taking a trial run at frugality, you should be able to ascertain whether your family will continue to thrive on the new budget and lifestyle. You may find that a part-time job (performed inside or outside the home) might be necessary for a while. (For tips on living on one income see chapter eight, "Life on a Budget.")

☐ Educate yourself on your company's policies regarding employees' leaving their employment. Follow all the rules, and know your legal rights.

☐ Read guidelines regarding payment for unused vacation, comp and sick days, and find out whether the company requires a certain amount of notice in order for you to receive payment for these unused days.

☐ Check your employee benefits to determine how long insurance coverage will last after you resign. Schedule routine check-ups for covered members of your family before benefits cease. If your company covers dental and vision care costs, head for the dentist and optometrist, too.

☐ Find out when you become vested in your retirement or employee savings plan. If you have only a few months before you are eligible for the full payment, it may be worth it to postpone leaving until after that date.

See if you are able to leave your money in the company's plan after you quit or whether you are required to roll over the funds into another tax-deferred entity.

☐ Pray. Don't underestimate the influence the Holy Spirit can have on your boss's reaction to and support for your decision. If you believe God has brought you to this crossroads, it can be exhilarating as you help set in motion the next phase of his plan.

### As You Resign

☐ Temper your approach to fit your boss's personality and your relationship. Is your boss precise? Make your reasons for resignation forthright and clear; quickly get to the point. Do you have an easy-going, friendly relationship built? Explain in a more personal manner: "As you know, I have been needing to make a change in my life for quite a while, and I feel this is the best move for me and my family."

☐ If you feel nervous, role-play your resignation with a friend or family member. Be prepared to be firm but not belligerent. Plan which possible questions you will answer and which you will deflect. Some inappropriate questions (like, "How can you do this to us?") shouldn't be responded to at all. Don't allow yourself to be drawn into a debate over whether or not you should leave or a discussion of the pros and cons of being a stay-at-home mom.

> **Your decision will reap rich dividends in your children's moral bank accounts.**

☐ Ignore dire predictions that you'll be wasting your life. Given the chance, some people will try to convince you that society will pass you by, a poor wretch of a woman lost in a misguided quest for meaningful motherhood. It won't, and you're not. You're a smart woman making a smart decision that's sure to reap rich dividends in your children's moral bank accounts. Hold on to that thought, and smile as you tap on your boss's door.

☐ Anticipate giving the standard two weeks' notice or a negotiated longer period of time. Be prepared to leave that day, however, just in case those negotiations don't go as well as you hope.

☐ Offer to work part time from home if you think it's the best scenario for your family. Have a written plan in hand, outlining your idea. In your pitch, discuss

☐ what duties you will perform

☐ how many hours per week you will be available

☐ how you will transmit information or products between your house and the workplace

☐ how much you will charge

☐ how it will benefit the company in terms of production and costs

Convince your boss there are smart, savvy women now at the company who would be even better employees if work schedules were flexed to allow them to care for their children, too. Point out the potential gold mine of educated, competent women presently at home full time because they were given an "either work on the company grounds or forget it" choice by their former employer.

If your boss responds favorably to the idea of your working from home but is still a little hesitant, try easing both sides into the new routine. For instance, cut one in-office day first. See how that goes in terms of steadying your finances, redistributing your former workload and achieving your boss's goals. After a predetermined amount of time, move to two days outside the office, then three, etc.

**After You Resign**

If your position doesn't have a written job description or basic manual outlining duties, develop one and submit it to your supervisor. This action projects you as a professional and shows your commitment to making the transition as smooth as possible. If you are planning to return to the same company after your children are older, devising this helpful guide for your replacement will remind your boss that you, too, care about the company's long-range goals. Keep a copy of the manual and save it for your future interview.

Here are some items you might like to include in the manual:

☐ a detailed list of responsibilities, with each duty described in clear terms and broken down step by step

☐ names, addresses and phone numbers of people you regularly work with (travel agents, suppliers, customers, company contacts, etc.—even your own phone number if you don't mind being asked a few questions once you're at home)

☐ an organizational chart showing supervisors and workers in various divisions and how the new hire's position fits into the overall company scheme

☐ sample copies of various forms regularly used, filled out as examples to follow

☐ an outline of the long-term goals of the department and how this position benefits the team

Now that the handbook has been prepared, finish as many outstanding projects as possible. Don't leave a mess for your successor or coworkers to clean up. Take some time over your last few days to train your replacement, maintaining a professional tone and refraining from sharing your opinions of your coworkers' attitudes or work habits.

☐ Be careful to balance any critical suggestions with praise in your exit interview. Don't take any final potshots. You risk shooting yourself in the foot, especially if you hope to work there again in the future.

## When Other Women Roar

Although you may be ecstatic about becoming a stay-at-home mom, remember that you are very likely surrounded by women with other things on their minds, including some who don't have any intention of leaving their outside jobs ever or couldn't even if they wanted to, due to circumstances beyond their control. In either case they don't want to hear about it.

A woman who has turned in her resignation so she can take time out to raise her kids may even discover that some coworkers openly denounce her decision. Unfortunately a stay-at-home mom's biggest critics are often other working women.

> Unfortunately a stay-at-home mom's biggest critics are often other working women.

You would think it would be just the opposite—that women would champion a sister's right to choose the avenue best suited to her. But there are women who feel that returning to a simpler lifestyle centered on home and family signals a weakening of women's rights in general, a slide backward into a chained-to-the-kitchen-sink mentality.

That's not the case, of course. Women who choose to become stay-at-home moms actually show exceptional strength of character. With all the options open to women it's not easy to deny yourself and put the needs of others first. Learning to live on one income is challenging. Breaking out of the mainstream and discovering an oasis of your own demands work and dedication.

Take heart. I suspect there are several other women in your office that have been struggling with the same issues you have. You can probably guess which ones—the woman watching the clock and then phoning home to make sure her child got off the bus safely . . . the red-eyed mother a couple of cubicles down who had to peel her toddler off her leg this morning and who's still replaying his screaming in her head . . . the women gathered around the break-room table talking about switching schedules and taking comp time to squeeze in a youngster's school performance. Your exodus may give these other women the confidence they need to make a similar move.

### Keeping Your Focus

When the reasons for your resignation become known around the office, expect several different reactions from your coworkers:

*Cheers and support* from those friends and kindred spirits who know your heart and who are glad to see you reach your goal of heading home. You're seen as a winner, someone who's gone for the gold and captured the prize. Some are living vicariously through you; others are right behind you, planning their own jump to home.

*Respect* from coworkers whose wives or mothers are or were stay-at-home moms and who appreciate the positive impact this move can make in a family. Often these supportive men and women will share some helpful tips on making the transition from the workplace to home and can suggest ways to network with other stay-at-home moms. Take advantage of their insights and resources.

*Grumbling* from coworkers who think they will have to pick up the slack while the company looks for your replacement. You're seen as a deadbeat who has just made their life harder and will probably be viewed as such no matter how hard you work until the last whistle sounds. Knowing this ahead of time can help you deal with the prejudice.

*Anxiety* from supervisors whose deadline pressures escalate as they seek to replace a valuable link in their production chain. These are the people who will try bargaining with you, offering you more money, better benefits—anything to get you to stay a little longer. Don't let their sweating sway you.

*Jealousy* from other working mothers who are either unwilling or unable to make the same choice for themselves. Steer clear of negativity and ignore any slighting remarks. There's no need to get into confrontations, especially when you realize that before you know it you'll be out of here! Thoughts of their grumbling will soon be crowded out by the memories you'll be making with your family.

You may not be able to do anything about jealousy, but you can take measures to limit the amount of coworker grumbling and anxiety. If at all possible finish assigned projects before your last day. Turn down any new, intricate projects you won't be able to get done. Train your replacement well, including providing a written set of instructions for routine tasks.

Keep a positive attitude, without saying too much around those who don't have the same opportunity. The way you act in these final weeks will influence the intensity of others' reactions.

As you approach the difficult task of informing your supervisor and then dealing with the results of your resignation, remember to keep your focus on the ultimate Boss. When we give our lives to Christ, the Bible says, it is no longer we who live but Christ who lives through us (Galatians 2:20). God has a job for us to do, and we need to be willing to do that job. If he's called you to work at home, being a hands-on mom who relays his training to the children he's given you, then you'd be crazy not to pick up your cradle and follow him. Think of it as a promotion.

# 7

## My Husband's Nervous; My Relatives Think I'm Crazy

THE FIRST TIME I TOLD TERRY I WANTED TO QUIT WORK, HE REACTED so abruptly our relationship fell headlong into an icy crevasse and stayed there a week.

His anger caught me off guard and, wounded, I immediately assumed—wrongly—that my husband didn't care about our kids as much as I did. Instead of a green light at this important life intersection, I got a hopping-mad crossing guard demanding, "Stop. Do not pass 'Go.' Do not turn in your resignation."

How could he say no? The pout was on.

What was your husband's reaction the first time you approached him with the idea of your quitting work and staying at home with the children? Elation? Reservation? Panic?

Even some men who wish their wives could devote themselves full time to home and family start sweating when they face the prospect of being the sole breadwinner. A generation ago men naturally assumed they would single-handedly provide financial support. But with the advent of two-income families that blanket assumption no longer exists. Now more husbands look at their wives as income-producing partners.

Some women run into second-generation resistance because of their spouse's own mother.

"My husband had a workaholic supermom," points out one lady who's having trouble convincing her husband she should quit work. "I think that's why he thinks it's a breeze for me to keep house, take care of the kids and still work more hours than God gives us in a day. He sees—or thinks he sees, as some other like-minded men do—that one income just doesn't work financially. Even if I don't make much money, at least it's flowing through the checking account.

"Now don't get the wrong idea. My husband is loving, committed, spiritual, etc. But he's got this hang-up that life's better when I'm working an outside job."

Yep. I understand the conflict. Classic miscommunication.

### Till Debt Do Us Part

In my own situation it turned out Terry was angry because he thought I was backing out of an unspoken deal I had made with him. All through dating and our early marriage I had pursued my degree and started a career. Counting on my continuing that career, Terry had joined me in racking up debt we could easily handle with both of us working—building a new house, driving new cars and using credit cards as freely as cash. Balances didn't bother us because we could handle the monthly payments.

Until I suddenly dropped my side of the safety net. Or so it seemed to Terry.

Because I didn't have a distinct plan when I first talked with him—I was basically dreaming out loud—my Pollyanna attitude and his fear of financial disaster clashed with a resonating clammor.

After a few days in the frozen food section, I cracked under his resistance. Of course he was right. What kind of a wife was I, threatening to undermine all the progress we had made as a couple? We weren't millionaires; there was no way we could live on one income. Yes, we both loved our girls, but facts were facts. I could not come home.

Over the next couple of years, the issue would occasionally resurface, but oddly enough, we never took out the calculator and got specific with the details. We fell into the two-working-parents routine, numbing emotions so we could leave our children in daycare for eleven hours a day. As I mentioned in chapter one, it took the head-on collision of a sick child and a work deadline to jolt us both into seeking our true options.

## Clearing Away Misconceptions

One of the reasons I wrote this book was to encourage prospective at-home moms to look at their options now without waiting for a crisis that may reveal a choice they could have taken two years before.

In actuality Terry and I had the ability to bring me home long before we realized we could. But I lost my husband when I talked in touchy-feely abstracts instead of in concrete here's-how-we-can-do-it terms.

When examined from a surface level it does appear that if you have two people working, you are making more money than if one person works. But this is not necessarily true. Yes you are *bringing in* more money. Whether or not you're *clearing* more money after expenses remains to be seen. By using elements of the business plan suggested in chapter three ("Setting Up Your Family Business Plan") and implementing cost-saving ideas listed in chapter eight ("Life on a Budget"), you'll be able to get a clearer picture of your family's true financial position.

> Yes you are bringing in more money. Whether you're clearing more money remains to be seen.

Once you've worked out the money details and can show your husband on paper how present cash flow can be revised to meet your family's needs even on one income, he'll probably be willing to hear more.

Can your family make it on just his income if you cut costs? Do you need to work part-time to maintain a standard of living you are both comfortable with? Can he pick up some overtime or change shifts to make the amount of money you need?

Even if your spouse is the only one working outside the home, he will not be supporting the family single-handedly. He'll bring home the paycheck, of course. But husband and wife work together to ensure that income is spent wisely. In reality, God has given your husband's job to the family as a whole; God is the one who really provides the cash. It's up to both of you to be good stewards of what God has provided.

### Involving the Whole Family

Now is the time to bring those bills under control. That may mean selling a car or two, or even putting an expensive home on the market and purchasing one with a mortgage that can be more easily handled within a proposed one-income budget.

"We have scaled back every possible expense and adjusted our lifestyle to prepare for me to be home," explains Shauna, the former French teacher I mentioned earlier. "My husband is completely supportive of my decision, and I love him dearly for it. We'll probably sell our new car. I know my wardrobe will become very familiar over the next several years, and I now wear Avon instead of Lancome.

"I know I'm not the only woman giving up the 'things' of life to choose what's really important," she continues. "I thought it would be harder to give up things that my friends in two-income families have, but it's surprising how much I really don't care about all that. Someone once said, 'Women can have it all, just not at the same time.' That phrase has been an inspiration to me."

It's also a good idea to let kids have input on some financial choices, too. Since the whole family will probably need to cut back, ask your sons and daughters to determine what they can live without and what is really important to them.

For example, when they're spending their parents' money, are they willing to settle for video parties with their friends in lieu of going to the movies every weekend? Will they graciously accept going to the lake this vacation instead of flying to Walt Disney World?

Present these choices in a positive light, where older children can feel they have done their part in bringing Mom home and can celebrate their own contribution toward this family goal.

### Pitching the New Routine

Beyond the financial concerns, a husband may be wondering what his wife will do all day long. So think that through too, before you talk with him.

Draw up a proposed schedule, showing planned activities with the kids, household tasks (divided between you and your spouse at a ratio you agree upon), time set aside for just the two of you, etc.

Remember as you devise this schedule that you have not taken on a new boss in the form of your husband. You are not giving him a checklist whereby he can grade your progress or nitpick. Instead you are sharing with him, your partner, a general outline for creating a wonderful home life for your children and a safe haven for him, too.

> **Never quit work without your husband's full support.**

Make a date to discuss your ideas, and get a friend to watch the kids so you two can talk without distractions.

I'm told we should never say *never,* but I feel so strongly about this that I must say it: Never quit work without your husband's full support.

There are too many godly working women connected with awesome biblical events—like Deborah (judge), Dorcas (seamstress), Lydia (dealer in purple cloth) and Priscilla (tentmaker)—for me to believe that all moms are being called on to leave the workplace.

All your persuasiveness and heartfelt conviction will bring about conflict in your marriage only if after you have presented a clear and detailed picture to him, you find your spouse doesn't feel the same way. I personally believe God would not call a wife to stay home when making that move would hurt her relationship with her husband.

If you are sure it is God encouraging you to become a stay-at-home mom, and you run into resistance from your mate, don't despair. Remember that you stand before God as one flesh, two individuals equally yoked for his glory. He's not going to send you each off in a different direction.

Instead of pouting, pray. The Holy Spirit is a great motivator, and I guarantee that if God wants you home, your husband's heart will soften and he'll begin to see the benefits you already know.

**Honoring Critical Parents**

"My mother-in-law acted like I was some kind of freeloader, turning her son into a slave so I could lounge around the house all day."

Unfortunately many stay-at-home moms can attest to the pain of this fictional quote.

More often, in-laws and parents aim at being supportive, but they inadvertently undermine their grown children's resolve by making inappropriate suggestions or observations. Some parents see their children's success as an extension of their own goals, so when their daughter decides to stay home, they view it as undermining their plans for the couple. Others would never come out and say they disapprove; instead they drop hints about all the time she's invested in her degree and ask when she's planning to go back to work.

> **Be prepared to deal with loved ones who don't see things the way you do.**

Whether it comes in the form of a gentle "sure was easier to make ends meet when you were both working" or a barbed comment like the "freeloader" statement above, you should be prepared to deal with loved ones who just don't see things the way you do.

If you choose to share some of the details of your plan with your parents or in-laws, they may be pleasantly surprised and relieved to see how your coming home will benefit your family; they may become supporters instead of adversaries.

It could be helpful for your husband to talk with his parents alone or for you to meet alone with your parents. However it is handled, you as a couple should make it gently but firmly understood that although you respect your parents, you have decided that in your family it's best for Mom to be home.

Sometimes, though, no matter how much talking you do, the tongue-wagging and head-shaking will continue. This is unfortunate because making the transition is difficult enough without having pressures from your family too. If you feel like some relatives are dragging you down, you may have to distance yourself from them a bit. I'm not advocating rebellion—just a little passive resistance.

Draw close to your husband and to God; if they're in your corner, you can confidently and calmly face opposition, whether it is rooted in love or in selfishness. Time is the best opinion-swayer on this subject anyway, as grandparents and aunts and uncles begin to see the fruits of your decision positively reflected in your children.

It may be too simplistic for me to say, "They'll get over it," but don't let the naysayers bother you. You don't have to defend yourself or account to anyone, especially someone that is looking to tear you down. God has a way of providing the restraint we need in dealing with irritating individuals, as long as we keep our eyes on him.

If you need a salve for your wounded ego, just reach out your arms and invite your children into your lap. They'll show you how they vote.

### Throwing Off the Shackles

There's no doubt that women were wrongly suppressed in the past and given few options for productive employment. No wonder some parties flame up at the notion of a smart, professional women "throwing it all away" to become an at-home mother. Their view of homemaking is skewed in such a way as to make dropping out of the workforce, even for a relatively short period of time, a tactical error.

Young couples starting their own families today are children of a generation in which women poured into the workplace in record numbers. Some of the resistance felt from these women, now grandparents, over the prospect of their daughters staying home is firmly rooted in the early 1970s mindset. These are formerly working mothers who went from being told they couldn't be boss to being told they had to dress like men to succeed to bumping their heads against the glass ceiling and then finally to knocking that barrier aside.

For their daughters or daughters-in-law to pipe up and say they want to go back home can seem like the ultimate betrayal.

I don't believe it is a wrong move, though, especially for those professional women who understand the importance a secure family structure plays in supporting all of the rest of society. What good does it do to build a thriving business community at the expense of the ultimate private sector—the family?

However you choose to present your plans to your relatives, know that more often than not people will follow the tone you set yourself. If you feel confident in choosing to stay home, let that assurance show.

> **A woman's place is wherever God calls her.**

Remember your kids are listening, too. You're giving the message to the next generation that a woman can be multifaceted, molding herself to succeed in various arenas, whether inside or outside the home. Your daughter's future vistas widen as she considers what to do with her life, and you'll expand your son's views about his own future role as a husband and father. With a little understanding we may all be able to agree that a woman's place is wherever God calls her.

### Easing Out of Daycare

Relatives are not the only ones who will need to be informed. You'll want to give your childcare provider plenty of notice of your decision to quit work too. Many daycare centers have waiting lists and will have no trouble filling your spot. Individual childcare providers, however, may need time to advertise their opening. Be considerate of your sitter's financial needs, as well as your own. If you have a written contract with your provider, be sure to follow its termination guidelines so you'll be able to get a refund of any deposits or prepayments.

If your child is sad about leaving his friends at daycare, assure him that you'll bring him back to visit. After I came home, about once a month I'd buckle Karen and Carrie in the van and take them by their old childcare center to see their favorite teachers and playmates. As time went on I stretched out the time between visits until Karen and Carrie were secure with their new friends and activities.

Prepare older children for any other changes that may affect them, such as catching a different bus and coming directly home after school instead of going to the sitter's. One benefit a new at-home mom and her school-age kids immediately reap is an additional two or three hours together each afternoon. I was amazed at how dinnertime frenzy diminished now that we had three to five o'clock free to finish homework, do chores and prepare for any evening activities.

Leslie, a Web-surfer mom, posted this on a messageboard: "One of the major improvements I have seen is when it comes to dinnertime. It used to be crazy! Either I or DH [short for *dear hubby*] would pick the kids up from daycare and meet at home. Then I'd hear the dreaded 'What's for dinner?'

"I certainly didn't feel like cooking. All I wanted to do was spend what little time I had with the kids. Of course, they were cranky. By the time dinner was made, everyone was cranky and dinnertime was awful. Then we had to clean up, and what do you know? It was time for bed because we had to have those kids up again by 6:30 a.m.

"Now that I'm home, dinner is almost always ready when DH walks in the door. We sit down to a relaxed meal and talk about the day. I think that has made us a much closer family.

"Of course I don't always feel like cooking, but I see this as part of my job now. I take care of the house. When the children have been extra difficult during the day, I deem it Pizza Night and I get the night off. DH usually cooks on the weekends to give me a break.

"I do want to mention that in no way does my husband expect dinner on the table when he gets home. Not a single night goes by that he doesn't thank me for cooking and for taking care of the family. Feeling appreciated sure makes this job a lot easier!"

Speaking of "dear hubbies," have you talked with your own about how chores will be redistributed once you come home? Is he assuming that with a stay-at-home wife he is getting a free pass and will never have to pick up a dishcloth again? Are you expecting the chore distribution to remain exactly the same, since you plan to be spending your extra time focused on your children instead of the vacuum cleaner? It's time for a heart-to-heart chat at your own kitchen table.

**Don't Forget About Yourself**

As you're working toward your goal of coming home, it's a good idea to link up with other like-minded women who have already made the transition. In the "Resources" appendix at the back of this book you'll find numerous support groups, including Mothers of Preschoolers, Formerly Employed Mothers at the Leading Edge and Moms in Touch, all devoted to encouraging stay-at-home moms. Consider attending a meeting or two at the local chapter of one of these organizations before you quit your job.

If visiting a group doesn't fit your present schedule, log on to one of their websites after work and participate in a chatroom discussion or leave an entry on a messageboard. Chatters generally communicate in an open, easygoing style, and most are eager to share their experiences to help working moms considering coming home.

Be on the lookout for a local mentor who will listen to your concerns and suggest some ideas for easing into your new lifestyle, too. Mentors are just as important on the home front as in the boardroom. How do you cultivate a relationship like this? See chapter sixteen ("Finding Your Mentor").

As in so many other facets of our lives, good communication skills help ease misunderstandings and tension. Keep those heartfelt talks going with your spouse, family and friends, mining the support you need from those close to you as you go through this thrilling and challenging transition period.

# 8

.........................

# Life on a
# Budget

**F**EAR OF FINANCIAL RUIN KEEPS MANY A DISCONTENTED MOTHER PLUG-
ging away at the office, even when she would rather pull up stakes and
head for her own backyard. It is true that for some women, most notably
single moms, staying home will have to remain a dream because the
monetary resources are simply not there.

However, the majority of prospective homemakers will be delighted to
find themselves embodying the proverb "where there's a will, there's a way."

Sacrifices made so a parent can stay home with the kids will, of course,
vary according to each family's circumstances. But the old adage "it's not
how much you make, it's how much you spend" is true! You would be
surprised how many ways to cut costs a determined stay-at-home mom
wannabe can discover.

This is not to say that I don't enjoy nice things. Of course I do. But I'm
not going to let those extras stand between me and my girls. What good
is a fabulous house that stands empty as my girls stay at another woman's
home while I work to pay the mortgage? That's crazy!

If you find yourself sulking as you consider giving up luxuries such as the one I've just mentioned, you're not ready to become a stay-at-home mom. If your husband balks at cutting back on expensive extracurricular activities like golfing or boating, give it up.

Unless you and your husband are equally committed to bringing you home, then—just like the fairy tale about the three little pigs—you're constructing your stay-at-home dream house out of straw. The first strong wind will blow your good intentions to smithereens.

But if both agree, there are exciting days ahead building that dream together, brick by brick. Just approach it with the same care and planning any worthwhile endeavor demands.

### Getting Your House in Order

Hopefully, before you turn in your resignation you've already implemented a family business plan like the one suggested in chapter three ("Setting Up Your Family Business Plan"). Credit cards have been paid down, you've got a comfortable cushion in your savings account for emergencies, and you've trimmed your installment loans to an easily manageable level.

Now it's just a matter of learning to live on the day-to-day reduced budget of a one-income family. If you continue to spend at the same rate you used to, the savings will disappear, the credit cards will roar back to life, and before you know it you'll be forced to return to work.

Not to worry. You *can* do this.

### Putting My Money Where My Mouth Is

I'll be happy to let you peek at my own stay-at-home mom's budget, to get some insight into living on one income. You may say, "Gee, that's a lot of work for such little return." Keep reading. Consistent cost-cutting over the broad scope of your finances can reap significant rewards.

Got your highlighter handy? All right. On your mark . . . get set . . . save!

As I mentioned before, when I first came home, we sold an expensive vehicle we had financed and bought a reliable older car for cash. Even with the occasional breakdown the overall cost was still less than making a regular monthly payment. And because we didn't owe any money on our autos, we chose to carry only liability insurance, which slashed our premium costs.

By securing a no-fee mortgage refinance, we cut our monthly house payment by 20 percent, with no out-of-pocket expenses. All it cost us was time—a few phone calls to go through the loan application process and then a short drive to the mortgage company to sign the papers.

A couple of years later we were debating a move to a different residence but decided to minimize costs instead by doing a little remodeling where we were. Terry and I took out a credit-union-financed home equity loan. Besides the remodeling, we used it to pay off a credit card balance that had crept up, as well as a couple of remaining installment loans. Interest was tax-deductible; we paid one bill instead of four and we're now enjoying a new home office—all for about a hundred dollars less a month than we were paying out before.

We raised the deductible amounts on our insurance policies, after shopping around to secure the lowest price on life, homeowner and car insurance. We chose comprehensive medical plans that limit out-of-pocket expenses and allow us to pay a flat rate per office visit.

## The Value of Being a Cheapskate

I continue to jealously guard my stay-at-home status by resisting paying full price for anything. I stick to that conviction while watching for coupons and weekly sales, taking stores up on their price-matching offers. By carrying three different ad flyers into a local department store, I save gas as I do all my shopping in one spot. Why drive around town to three department stores when a store close by will match their prices?

There is usually a thirty-day price guarantee too. After making your purchase, watch advertisements over the next month. If the item you bought goes on sale, you can visit the service desk with your proof of purchase and get a cash refund for the difference between what you paid and the new price.

I don't go to the mall unless I'm carrying a sale flyer that places items within my limited budget. When buying big-ticket items from commissioned salespeople, I always negotiate over price. You'd be surprised how

> **Be wise as a serpent, gentle as a dove . . . and demand the best deal available.**

many sticker prices are negotiable. You probably already know you can haggle over cars, but what about furniture? or appliances? Anywhere there's a commission to be made, there's a salesperson who has a vested interest in selling you something. Be wise as a serpent, gentle as a dove . . . and demand the best deal available.

I know of a jewelry store where, for instance, the price you pay depends upon the rank of your salesperson. The higher the rank, the more flexibility they have in negotiating. Ask for the store manager—managers are authorized to give you the best deal. If you are buying an especially expensive item or are a regular customer, make an offer and ask the store manager to pass it on to the owner.

When shopping for groceries, make a detailed list before you leave the house and stick to it. Make sure you've eaten, too, so irresistible goodies don't leap into your basket. Take coupons for the items you've selected, and patronize supermarkets that give you double and triple their face value. Invest in a freezer and stock up on "loss leaders"—the low-priced teaser items stores use to lure you in.

Also use coupons when dropping coats, suits and dresses off at the cleaners. Know your fabrics; many clothes marked "dry clean only" can be hand washed in gentle soap for delicates and turn out just fine. Handling these items yourself will cut your costs. But a sure way of saving money is by avoiding buying "dry clean only" clothes in the first place!

Speaking of buying clothes, don't overlook those neighborhood garage sales, especially the ones held in more upscale areas of town. Kids grow out of clothes so quickly that these sales can be a blessing. Often gently worn jeans and pristine dresses are found for pennies. You can also garner some cash and free up space by cleaning out closets and basements for your own sale.

Our credit union offers no-cost checking. By purchasing checks through the mail I pay a third of what banks are charging. For that inevitable loan I've found credit unions consistently charge lower rates than banks, so they've got my business when it comes time to buy a big-ticket item on time payments.

We paid off, then canceled, all our credit cards except one. This major credit card is at a low fixed rate and has no annual fee. We aim to use our card only to the extent that we can pay it off each month, avoiding debt and interest charges. If you have an excellent credit history, ask for your annual fee to be waived. There's a good possibility they'll agree, since competition for trustworthy credit customers is fierce.

To keep spending in line you might consider using a debit card, which works like a check. It draws only on the funds you currently have in your account. That way you're not borrowing against future earnings.

The first time I stroked out on opening an outrageously high summer electric bill, I called the utility company and learned about level payment plans. Now we pay a predetermined amount each month, protected from high charges generated by July's heat or January's freezing temperatures.

Take advantage of buy-in-bulk opportunities on everything from frozen foods to Internet access service. (One year, by paying for a year in cyberspace upfront, I locked into an $11.95 per month rate when most of my friends were paying $19.95.)

Send e-mail messages to online friends and associates instead of calling long distance or using snail mail. Speaking of postage, I don't put a stamp on any mail I can deliver myself.

**Go for the Freebies**

Fill out and mail those rebate forms. In the past year, I've received a scanner, a computer modem, 200 diskettes, 16 mb memory, mechanical pencils, ink pens, colored markers, three desk organizers, several ring binders and a software upgrade for free, just because I took the time to fill out the proper paperwork.

Often I'll come out ahead when using a combination of coupons and mail-in rebates. For instance, a shampoo was on sale for $2.50. I used a 50 cent coupon, and this store doubled it. My cost for the shampoo was now $1.50. I took two minutes to fill out the $2.00 mail-in rebate attached to the bottle. Even after the cost of a 32-cent stamp I had a free bottle of shampoo and 18 cents to the good.

I don't pay for baby-sitting when I can trade with a friend. But when this option is not available and I'm strapped for cash, I try not to let the daunting dollar tally of dinner plus movie plus sitter ruin our plans. Rather than nixing an evening out, I try negotiating with my sitter, asking her to accept a flat rate: for instance, five hours for the price of four. You can try this, too. The sitter may see the advantage in accepting less as opposed to missing out completely on her own movie money. Be sure to reward your sitter by having a special treat available for her and the kids, or thank her after a future assignment by paying a little extra to compensate for her flexibility now.

A film fanatic, I've been known to trade typing services for movie tickets. I frequent half-price matinees and AMC theaters because I have an AMC MovieWatcher card. I earn discounts and points toward free food and tickets every time I go. MovieWatchers also get free popcorn on Wednesdays. So guess which is my favorite day to take the kids to the movies?

I only attend movies I'm dying to see. All others I rent on video—when specials are running at the video store, such as two for the price of one.

Whether minding our manners at a sit-down restaurant or pigging out at the local buffet, my family uses newspaper coupons and coupon books. Sometimes it's cheaper to eat out than cook at home, especially when you visit an establishment where kids eat free.

One example is a local restaurant which allowed two children to eat free on Wednesdays, with one adult purchase. Since there was no minimum amount of purchase, I could select a sandwich and fries (under four dollars) and the kids could hit the all-you-can-eat buffet. It would have cost me much more than four bucks to prepare a comparable dinner at home.

We ate great, and I didn't have to cook or clean up. Since we were on our way to Wednesday-night church anyway, we didn't have any extra fuel costs, either. It was a winner of a situation, especially since it gave me one less thing to worry about—preparing dinner—on a traditionally busy evening.

Penny-pinching aside, there are some things you just gotta have. After trying to live without it for six months, our family decided satellite TV, with its classic movies, round-the-clock sports and cartoons, was something we valued too much to miss. So we'll cut somewhere else.

Instead of taking a daily newspaper, I buy the Sunday paper, which usually pays for itself because of the numerous coupons inside. I don't purchase books or magazines I can check out of the library, unless I can use the information in them on an ongoing basis.

## Look and Learn

Networking is important. Find out whose brother-in-law works on home computers . . . whose friend knows lawns . . . whose sister holds a once-a-year primo garage sale with designer outfits going for a pittance.

Don't pay someone else to do something you can do yourself. Learn to confidently maintain your automobiles, do your own taxes, perform your own repairs. Wear out your library card checking out "how-to" books.

The secret to pruning your budget is mastering the ability to separate wants from needs. Putting your family on a financial diet has the potential of producing the healthiest parent/child relationship you've ever enjoyed.

By applying thrifty principles liberally, you'll be surprised how much you'll save. Then when it comes time to splurge on something that's just pure fun, you won't feel guilty—it'll be your reward for being such a good steward of your finances.

> **Don't pay someone else to do something you can do yourself.**

# 9

·······················

# God, the Ultimate Money Manager

**M**ID-OCTOBER LOOMED BEFORE US LIKE AN IMPENETRABLE GRAY fog. Every three years the union contract at the steel company where Terry worked came up for renewal. No matter how well business had been going, each time pending discussions between labor and management brought about distrust and discord, straining previously cordial relationships.

Terry and I were well-versed in running our one-income household on a shoestring. After working full-time for most of my adult life, we had shifted priorities a year earlier and determined I would stay home with my youngest daughter, Carrie, now three. Her big sister, Karen, was attending second grade, and I was enjoying recapturing my spot in their daily lives.

There were few frills, but our priorities were set. The Chevy Impala and decade-old truck sitting in our driveway weren't flashy, but their well-maintained chassis got us where we were going. The money that used to go for a car payment now assured Karen a spot in the local Christian school.

Always a shrewd bargainer, I had honed my money-saving skills and was dangerously close to becoming a miser. If it wasn't on sale or if I didn't have a coupon, we probably didn't need it. Wal-Mart began to look expensive as I discovered treasures in neighbors' garage sales. Friends chuckled as I excitedly shared my best finds: "You like my sweater? I got it for a dime!" I bartered and I cut costs; I managed our money down to the last penny. There was certainly no room in our budget for extravagances like tithing.

> There was no room in our budget for extravagances like tithing.

Already pulled financially as far as we could stretch, a strike was the last thing our family needed. With his fortieth birthday just a couple of years away and his future in jeopardy, Terry found himself in the throes of a midlife crisis. Finally, after days of struggling, Terry came to a decision.

"It's time to look for another job."

I was dumbfounded. Terry was not naturally given to change. I had encouraged him to switch to a more settled profession several times over the course of our marriage, but he had always resisted.

"I know I'm making good money now, enough so you can stay home with the girls. But I hate this. I need a job with more stability. I want to be a full-time truck driver," he asserted. "And I'm praying that the Lord will open up the right opportunity."

Terry began interviewing. Before each phone call, we prayed. As Terry traveled to meet with a prospective employer, he knew I was at home praying. Glittering offers of more money danced before us, then were rejected as we realized that for one reason or another, the family would suffer if Terry took the job.

One day Terry spotted an ad in the newspaper. A small steel firm was in need of a truck driver. Although he had sworn off steel companies, he decided to check out the fledgling nonunion business.

He came away from the interview with mixed feelings. Although the job itself seemed perfect, the pay was not. At almost 30 percent less than his prior salary, Terry thought as solitary breadwinner he should not pursue it. But he continued to feel drawn toward the company.

"God, if this is not the job, please let them be lukewarm or standoffish when I call them back."

The next morning Terry called the interviewer, who enthusiastically suggested that Terry meet with him and the owner. There was no trace of hesitation in the interviewer's voice—only great hopes for the future.

That night Terry and I prayed again. "God, you know the money is just not there. But we're asking for your guidance. If you want Terry to work with this company, please show us clearly your will."

The evening was filled with wonderful, heartfelt conversation between husband and wife. I realized that for God's hands to be untied to work unencumbered in Terry's job situation, I had to be willing to submit to God's will, whatever it was.

And that meant being willing to go back to work, if necessary.

The meeting with the owners the next day lasted more than two hours. As I anxiously waited at home, praying almost constantly, I tried to calm my heart, wondering what God would work out. What was going on? Was the meeting going on so long because they really liked him?

*Surely these owners realized they needed to pay more to hold on to the best worker they had ever met. After all, God knew I needed to be home with my girls.*

Or had the meeting been short and sweet, a friendly parting of the ways, and Terry was now out getting something to eat, forgetting to call his frazzled wife?

When Terry finally got home, he told me the owners were just as enthusiastic as the interviewer about him driving for their company. Disappointingly, there was no increase in salary; the pay was the best they could offer at this time. However, something extraordinary had happened.

One of the owners had approached Terry as he was preparing to leave. "The way you talked during the interview leads me to think you might be a Christian." When Terry affirmed that he was, the owner astounded him by saying he was, too, and he had been praying for a truck driver.

As Terry related the conversation, awareness of God's will washed over both of us. "I don't think it can get any plainer than this." I agreed.

**Tough Times Settle In**

I went over the figures again. The result was the same—Terry's first paycheck from his new job would not cover our bills.

Silently, I rose from the table. Standing at the dining-room window, I stared outside gloomily at the barren November landscape. *I've been a fool. I never really believed I would have to go back to work.*

*Surely,* I mused, *something would happen to adjust the math, to right the figures that had been so plain when Terry and I decided to make his job change.* Thirty percent was a devastating loss in our family's budget, and no amount of belt-tightening or cost-cutting would compensate. I had to go back to work.

*How could the Lord snatch away my unfettered time with my children?*

Even as these thoughts arrived, they were dispelled by God's gentle spirit. I had already had a year, much longer than many of my friends had ever had with their children. Maybe through his God-given job, Terry would be able to influence someone to accept Christ, someone who might otherwise have been lost. I kept trying to find a rational explanation, even if it existed only in a nebulous, mysterious future.

Over the next few days, grieving gave way to acceptance and acceptance to anticipation, as I began to consider God's will for me. Just as we had prepared for Terry's search, we now prayed for God's guidance in finding my job. The number-cruncher in me had determined that if I could just clear so much a week, we could squeak by—but I still hadn't included a tithe in the budget.

*It's not going to be so bad after all,* I reasoned. *I could just work part-time.*

I decided to network purely among Christian friends and see what turned up. Amazingly, four solid leads appeared almost immediately, and I thanked God.

In the midst of this interviewing period, Karen's school called. The daycare provider's grandson was ill, and they needed someone to fill in for a couple of days. Would I be interested?

Normally, I wouldn't have been, because the pay was so low. But at this stage, we were so broke that any money was welcome. So I took on the role of preschool teacher while I waited to hear back from my interviews.

A couple of days later, the school called again. One of the teachers was out; would I like to substitute? That would be great. I could use the extra money, especially since I had been turned down after two job interviews.

Once again, the school contacted me. There was a before- and after-school daycare position open. "I'll be glad to help you out until I get a job," I said. So I found myself playing Hangman and Charades with the elementary students and discovered I loved it.

### Waylaid by Malachi

As the days stretched on, our monetary situation became more and more precarious. On Sunday, we attended church.

"Will a man rob God? Yet you rob me."

"How do we rob you?"

"In tithes and offerings."

Pierced to the heart, I sat rigidly in the pew. Here I was, a Christian for more than twenty years, listening to my thousandth tithing message, and for the first time, the words of Malachi slapped me right in the face.

A Bible-study leader, a coordinator for a support group for stay-at-home moms, a person who had experienced God's wonderful healing powers, a staunch defender of Christ—yet Jesus had one thing against me. Just like the rich young ruler in Luke I had refused—no matter how politely—to turn over my money. You see, I had decided long ago that it was skinflint churches that promoted tithing. And putting in my two-cents worth wasn't as heavenly ordained as it was pushed by preachers needing to make their car payments.

> I had decided long ago it was skin-flint churches who promoted tithing.

So as the years rolled by, I periodically put something in the plate whenever I felt generous. And by the same standard, when times were tough, I figured making my house payment was at least as important as helping the pastor make his.

God, in his infinite wisdom, decided to wait until our family was on the brink of financial disaster to make his point. "I the LORD do not change." There went my "it's just the Old Testament" excuse. "You are under a curse," the prophet continued. "The whole nation of you—because you are robbing me. Bring the whole tithe into the storehouse."

Then, just like the Jesus I've come to know and love, he softened his tone and said, "Test me in this . . . and see if I will not throw open the floodgates of heaven and pour out so much blessing that you will not have room enough for it" (Malachi 3:10).

Overwhelmed, I left the service and went home. All through dinner and the afternoon, the pastor's words spun in my head. How in the world were we supposed to come up with another 10 percent when we were already down by 30?

During prayer time with the Bible study group that evening, I broke down. "I need to say this out loud so I'll be accountable to someone." I hesitated; this was harder to talk about than sex. "The tithing message this morning hit me right between the eyes." Terry began to smile; he had been trying to convince me for more than a year that we should get serious about tithing.

"I don't know where he's going to get the money, but I want you to know that I have made a commitment to give God 10 percent of our income. Now, God," I looked at the ceiling, "you know what a bad witness it will be if we pay you but not our light bill. So I'm trusting you to provide. Thank you."

Two days later, I was shocked, humbled and then honored when I opened our mail and found a seventy-five-dollar gift certificate for a local supermarket in an unmarked envelope.

"God," I prayed, "bless whoever sent this for listening to your voice and sending this much-needed money. Because I know this is directly from you, I thank you so much. Please give whoever sent this five times as much back because of their obedience to you."

A few days later, when the money had run out but the month hadn't, we cashed the certificate and gratefully stocked our cabinets.

### God Provides
With the change in Terry's job, we found ourselves facing December with two unanticipated bills—one for health coverage to fill the gap during the probationary period and the other for personal property taxes. Through

diligent premium shopping I was able to find coverage for our family for $169. Taxes on our antiquated vehicles amounted to only $72.31, but since we had no money, it might as well have been a thousand.

Already wondering how we would pay these two bills, I was struck with terror when Terry remarked that we had received a letter from the IRS. Opening it, he found a surprise—a letter saying a mistake had been made on our income taxes and we would soon be receiving a check for $241.72. You do the math. (I wonder what the extra 41 cents is for!)

True to God's Word, the blessings were already beginning to pour.

"Well, the last door has closed," I sighed. It was Tuesday, a little over a week since a few verses from Malachi had changed my life. My last two prospective employers had called, one wanting me to work full time instead of part time (which I declined, still protective of my time with my children) and the other saying they had postponed filling the position until after the first of the year.

I began telling Terry about some antics the kids at school had pulled, laughing as I related some humorous incident. As I spoke, I realized how much I enjoyed working with the elementary students.

"If only the school paid better . . ." I started, and then immediately countered, "Well, that's a lack of faith!" so strongly I surprised myself.

The next day I was back at school, helping out while the secretary was on medical leave. The principal stepped into the office and asked if I would talk with him for a few minutes. Curious, I followed him. On his desk was a copy of my résumé.

"We've been looking for a part-time computer teacher, and I think we've had the perfect candidate under our noses all along," the principal said. As he proceeded to outline duties, hours and salary, tears welled up in my eyes.

I qualified for the position. The limited hours were perfect. And the salary not only covered our bills but included enough extra to pay not only my tithe but also my husband's, almost to the dollar.

" 'Test me in this,' says the LORD Almighty, 'and see if I will not throw open the floodgates of heaven and pour out so much blessing that you will not have room enough for it.' " (Malachi 3:10).

# 10

······················

# Avoiding Super
Stay-at-Home-Mom
Syndrome

LYING AT THE BOTTOM OF MY CHEST OF DRAWERS, HIDDEN AWAY FROM
inquisitive kids and husbands who just wouldn't understand, is a size 2
Toddler Easter dress. Let me be truthful and rephrase that. There are *pieces*
of a size 2 Toddler Easter dress.

These various pieces look especially impressive because I cut them out
using a pair of those zigzaggedly scissors that make you look like you know
what you're doing. Unfortunately, my sewing expertise sputtered out soon
after, as I started trying to decipher the inscrutable pattern directions.

Before I could intersect with the interfacing, I found I was unable to
salvage the selvage. Spools spun off the top of the machine, needles broke,
and the only thing I wanted to know about naps was when I could take
one.

Are you lost? Me too.

So I stuffed my forty dollars' worth of material, lace and shiny buttons
in that bottom drawer and headed for Wal-Mart. A couple of hours later,

Carrie was spinning around the living room in a fabulous new Easter dress that cost half of what I'd spent on my ill-fated frock.

That was four years ago. Since I don't have any more daughters and there's no way to recut a size 2 Toddler into a size 6X, I guess I've missed my window of opportunity. But I just can't seem to make myself toss that pile of pretty piecework.

### And She Shall Be Called Wonderful

When I first came home, I decided it was my duty to do everything from scratch. This is a ridiculous concept, of course. I don't remember walking into my first job and demanding a boulder and chisel instead of a typewriter. So why did I think I had to sew my own clothes, bake my own bread and quilt my own bedspreads?

> You're a stay-at-home mom, not a stay-at-home maid.

Don't worry that you'll slide off the Susie Homemaker scale if you attempt the same activities with disastrous results. Leave fretting over which detergent gets whites the brightest to those fictional ladies on TV. Instead decide on a few new tasks you'd like to master, not because of some perfect mother mental image but because you really want to learn this particular skill and you have an affinity for it.

### Tackling the Tricky Transition

"When I first started working, my house and everything was easy to handle because I didn't have this variable of kids," remembers Julie, who used to do department store visual merchandising. "When the boys came along and I was working, there were still these eight or nine hours a day when they weren't around to mess it up. There was a limit to the damage that could be done in the hour in the morning and three hours at night we were all home.

"Now that I'm here all the time, I've had to choose my battles. House-work is not a meticulous thing for me anymore; it's in a constant state of metamorphosis. Marshall toddles through the house with a trail behind him, a regular little Pigpen. I may trip over a lot of stuff, but he's a gentle child. And when he and Levi want to cuddle up with me, who cares if I haven't dusted in two weeks?

"My house might be piled with art stuff and unfinished projects, and last night's dinner dishes might be soaking in the sink. But my kids know they're loved, they know who God is, and they're careful in how they treat other people. In a few years they'll be gone to school and I'll have hours to clean. Right now I'm more concerned with their clean character than a clean house."

The point is to be a stay-at-home mom, not a stay-at-home maid. Stacie, who served in the spit-shine U.S. military, remembers her first few months home. "I thought I would have so much time on my hands that my house would be spotless. I had visions of clean laundry, dinner on the table and the kids lined up at the door with kisses for Daddy when he got home. I found out real quick that's not how it's going to be."

"It's really easy to fall into the June Cleaver syndrome," warns Erin, a physical therapist who decided to stay home with her son, Kurtis. "You've got eight to ten hours a day, but you're spending most of your time teaching and training a child. You can't do that when you're doing the more outwardly visible things like cooking and cleaning.

"It took me a long time to come to the realization that the dirt's not going anywhere, and really, it's not hurting anything. I have to admit, it's a constant battle for me, because I'll go back into that frenzy. But then I'll have this beautiful house with gourmet meals all week, and my son is cranky because he's paid for it."

### Setting Your Family's Internal Clock

"There's going to be an adjustment period for both you and your husband," says Stacie. "You might think, 'There must be something wrong with me, because it's not coming together yet.' But it takes time to fall in the right niche for you and your family."

One California mom was surprised at the initial conflict that erupted between her and her husband. "His mom was a servant to the family. That's what he saw growing up, and so that's what he expected. I was raised differently. My mom was home too, but my parents had more of a fifty-fifty operation. She handled secretarial work for my dad's business too, and they were a team.

"Our big problem was that my husband would walk through the door at the end of the day and wonder why everything wasn't done. 'You just stay home, so why aren't all the bills paid, the groceries bought, the house picked up, etc.' I may have just handled fifteen problems, and the last thing on my mind is what he wants for dinner. Sometimes I'm as exhausted as he is after a day swinging a hammer.

"I try to make him realize that all the things I do have a monetary value, just like the things he does, even though we don't see a paycheck from me. How much would it cost to hire an accountant to take care of all our bills, someone to clean the house, someone to take care of the kids? I'm homeschooling, too; how much would it cost for an outside tutor?"

Thankfully, this couple was eventually able to work out their differences and balance their expectations of each other. But their experience is not unusual. It is easy for spouses to get caught up in conflicting role issues when perfectionistic tendencies on either the wife's or husband's part have not been tackled before she quits her job.

"Some women feel like they're lousy moms because they're working," says Miriam, who left her secretarial position and started her own business at home. "Then they get home, and they feel like they're lousy moms because they still can't get everything done. If you had realistic goals when you were working, you're going to transfer that ability to your home life.

"It's just like when you get married. You think things are going to be a certain way, but they're not. Here's the deal: if you were holding on to the Lord when you were working, then hopefully you're still holding on to him at home. Basically you're the same personality working under different conditions.

"If you've quit your job out of guilt but not out of conviction, you're probably not going to have a successful stay-at-home mom experience. But if you're home because the Lord has changed your heart, you'll still have up and down days, but you'll be successful because you'll know you've made the right decision."

## Lightening Up

Since her first child was born, Elaine has always been home. Her goal was to be the ideal mom, doing the appropriate things to raise her children right and curbing wrong attitudes. "I thought I had to be perfect. Inside I knew I wouldn't be, but I wanted to strive for it. When I didn't reach (perfection), I was hard on myself. If I raised my voice, disciplined when angry . . . did those sorts of things, . . . I would feel extra bad.

"It's interesting to me now that some things are just not as important as I once thought. Things like having the kids behave well in public when they were younger. Now I realize, this too shall pass."

Jennifer learned to relax, too. This Kansas City mom jokes about her "mother-in-law drawer," an empty kitchen cabinet she can sweep messes into when the doorbell rings unexpectedly. "There's always the oven, of course. But I've left plastic things in there and regretted it. My husband will come to me holding a cockeyed spatula, going, 'What happened to this?'"

"In the beginning I thought I had to have everything ready by the time Jeff got home," remembers Dana, whose daughter, Sammi, is two. "But I eventually realized I couldn't keep up, and other women I talked to said the same thing. Jeff and I discussed what we expected from each other. By coming home I took on more household responsibilities but didn't have to take on as much as I thought.

"I used to be adamant about disinfecting the kitchen and bath every morning. And if I saw a spot on a window, I had to clean every single window. But I decided to draw up a schedule instead, to set certain days I would do that.

"I make lists, writing down the most menial things. When I cross things off, it makes me feel like I've accomplished something. Time management is the biggest thing. If the baby gets sick or something comes up, prioritize what you had planned and spread it out. Don't cram all today's

> Devise a schedule you can loosely adhere to.

duties into the next day; filter it through the week. Drop things that aren't
important."

"Figure out two or three things you will do every day," says Stacie. "Be
open-minded and don't be so hard on yourself. Devise a schedule for you
and the kids, something you can loosely adhere to. For instance, 'sometime
between 11:00 a.m. and 2:00 p.m., the baby's going down for a nap,' instead
of 'nap at 1:15 p.m.' "

"I try to find the joy in just being with the kids every day," says Julie.
"If that means taking a hour to make Spaghetti O's because my two-year-
old wants to get the can, turn on the can opener, help stir, etc., I'll do that.
It would go a lot quicker if I didn't let him do it, but my mom was a
hands-on mom. And I am too."

### Setting Perfectionism Aside

Let's join these loosed women and cut ourselves some slack. Why should
we put more pressure on ourselves than God does?

Look at Micah 6:8, and then absorb its meaning for a stay-at-home
mom:

> He has told you, O mortal, what is good;
>   and what does the LORD require of you
> but to do justice, and to love kindness,
>   and to walk humbly with your God? (NRSV)

I don't see a word in there about dishes.

As I finger the zigzagged pieces of my unfinished toddler dress, I know
I'm not really looking at failure. A lot of love went into this little frock,
even if it didn't turn out as perfectly as I had hoped. I start to put it in the
Goodwill bag, then inspiration strikes.

*I've got it! I'll save it for my first grandchild. Surely I will have figured out
fasteners by then.*

*Nah.* Showing some self-control, I wrap up the pattern and pieces to
give to charity. Let's see if some other mother out there is a gifted
seamstress. Meanwhile, I've got some SpaghettiOs to dish up with Carrie.

# 11

·······················

# A Fruitful
# Motherhood

SO HERE YOU ARE. YOUR HUSBAND'S OFF TO WORK. FRIENDS AND RELA-
tives are busy scaling their own personal Mt. Everests. A pair of sparkling,
inquisitive eyes is focused on you, wondering what's up next with Mommy.

It may sometimes feel like you're single-handedly lugging your child's
world around on your shoulders, but that's not true at all. You've got an
invisible coworker, a Friend who sticks closer than a brother. You've heard
of the Holy Spirit, a comforter and secret-whisperer sent straight from God.
He'll ease you through the tough days as an at-home mom and celebrate
the good ones with you, too.

I love this passage from Galatians 5:22-23: "But the fruit of the Spirit is
love, joy, peace, patience, kindness, goodness, faithfulness, gentleness and
self-control."

Here's a chance to put away scholarly interpretations and see how the
Word of God can become alive and active right in your own home. Take
God up on his offer to produce these qualities—the fruit of the Spirit—in
you as you raise your little ones.

## Love

"You assume that you love your kids," says Bonnie, who's raising four children while working from her home. "But then if I go back to 1 Corinthians 13 and read . . . well, maybe I'm not loving them in the God-intended sense of the word."

First Corinthians 13:4-8 says: "Love is patient, love is kind. It does not envy, it does not boast, it is not proud. It is not rude, it is not self-seeking, it is not easily angered, it keeps no record of wrongs. Love does not delight in evil but rejoices with the truth. It always protects, always trusts, always hopes, always perseveres. Love never fails."

The love you have for your children is your most important tool in raising them. You'll be amazed how that affection deepens as you spend more time together. This is one season when your life really should revolve around your kids.

"The years I had lost with Amber were restored," says Becky, who quit work when her daughter was seven. "When I was working, I felt my time with her was being stolen. That bond you have with your baby starts at birth, and it was tough. But since I've come home, we've become much closer as she's growing up."

"I am enjoying my time with Sammi," says Dana. "I think everything she does is amazing and brilliant. I just don't understand sometimes why people aren't as amazed at her obviously advanced behavior as I am! She's great—and so is her daddy; I can't forget him."

It is said that love covers a multitude of sins. It's true; your kids don't expect you to be perfect. The affection you show them registers higher than any expensive trinket you could buy with that bonus check you used to get from your company.

Openly express your love for your husband around your children, too. Set the tone to create a haven where the whole family can find acceptance and security through mutual love and respect.

## Joy

Have you ever tried to *make* somebody have fun? Working parents do it all the time. "What do you mean, you don't feel like it? I took this afternoon off just for you! I don't have any more time coming for two months, so get over it. Stop crying!"

Like the bumper sticker says, If Mama ain't happy, ain't nobody happy. But as an at-home mom you have the opportunity to minimize those less-than-joyful times. Storm clouds may appear on the day of the scheduled big event, but they rarely completely scuttle plans. Keep your upbeat attitude and come up with a Plan B to entertain expectant kids. Doing what? Check out chapter twelve, "Creativity on the Home Front," for some ideas. And with your new, more flexible schedule, there's a good chance you'll be able to reschedule the outing for a better day.

**There are challenges, sure. But in the midst of it all, make sure there's joy.**

Kids love a joyful parent. Just look at the way they respond to those silly song books. Or those incessantly jolly VeggieTales guys. Or those ridiculous Dr. Seuss characters, hopping and popping all over.

So your omelet's flat and your bacon's a little crispy. Shrug it off with a smile. I suspect the kids will be just as happy with cereal and milk. There are challenges, sure. But in the midst of it all, make sure there's joy.

## Peace

"I felt so free, as though a heavy chain had dropped off," remembers Becky. "I was able to do more Bible study, to pursue more spiritual growth in my walk with the Lord.

"It fulfilled me to quit work. Instead of being a nervous wreck, wondering how I'm going to fit everything in, now I can totally devote myself to my family. We went through a door that was very challenging, but when I got home, God kept everything going.

"It was incredible. When you know God's in something and you're right there with him, it's so fun to watch him work."

I know becoming a stay-at-home mom has extended my Type A, previously stroke-prone life. I was always so caught up in office politics and those crazy little irritations that sent my blood boiling. In fact, as I was visiting my former coworkers one day, I overheard some serious grumbling over an insignificant event. Honestly, I think it was something like "She never resets the copier, refills the paper bin, blah, blah, blah."

As I felt myself becoming agitated, I realized I hadn't felt like this in months. When I was a full-time working mom, I used to get fired up every single day. Then, my resistance was worn down by too many responsibilities on too many fronts. Peace was nonexistent.

It was good to see my friends again, but I couldn't wait to get back to my peaceful home!

As you contemplate leaving your job, there will be people all around trying to sway you from making that move. But if you're positive God is calling you to be a stay-at-home mom, then don't be anxious about anything. The "peace of God, which transcends all understanding, will guard your hearts and your minds in Christ Jesus" (Philippians 4:7). That's a promise straight from God's Word.

**Patience**
Some of the fruits of the Spirit are easier to say yes to than others.

"For me, love, joy, and peace were easy," says Elaine, whose three children range in age from six to eighteen. "Patience is a little harder."

I downloaded one of those great, uncredited humor pieces that are so numerous on the Net. "The Toddler Diet" had me rolling, as it described how two-year-olds keep their slim physiques: toddlers never really eat anything but lint and sand off sticky suckers thrown on the floor and picked up again two hours later. They may ingest an occasional Cheerio, but everything else is just smeared in their hair, on the high chair or on the dog. Oh, yeah, they love to eat dog hair, too. Yuck!

When you think of all the ways a child can mess up . . . well, maybe it's better not to think about it. It's best to take it one day at a time. That's where this gift of patience comes in handy.

Yes, there are times when willful disobedience kicks in. But more often than not, plain old immaturity is what puts kids on a collision course with their parents. They have their own gift of discovering creative ways to get in trouble without really meaning to.

I personally made it to adulthood without inserting a peanut butter sandwich in the VCR. But then, VCRs weren't around when I was five. I do know firsthand, however, what happens when you beat the dust out of a rug on the clothesline with a baseball bat. I meant well, but there still was a gaping hole in our neighbor's rug after my final swing.

As Art Linkletter points out, kids say—and do—the darnedest things. Thank God for the gift of patience; we're gonna need it.

### Kindness

Compassion is crucial when dealing with the bumps and scrapes, both physical and emotional, that kids are bound to suffer. No matter how they are treated elsewhere, children—and their fathers—need to know they have a safe place to come home to. Mom can help create that atmosphere for them.

> Children—and their fathers—need to have a safe place to come home to.

Proverbs 15:1 assures us that a gentle answer turns away wrath. "It's really easy to speak kindly to everyone else and then snap at our kids," says Debi, a freelance writer and at-home mother. I could hear Debi's son, Andrew, in the background, rambunctiously emulating Zorro as she and I talked on the phone. I waited for the inevitable "Stop that!" before our chat could resume.

Instead, Debi gently asked her son to quiet down, which he did, and returned to the conversation at hand. "James 1:20 says human anger does not bring about the righteous life that God desires. So getting mad and yelling will not bring about the attitude and character we want in our children. Kindness will."

Cultivating kindness in children, and then seeing that gentle spirit revealed as they work with others, is rewarding beyond words. Though you may never piece together a quilt or crochet a delicately embroidered tablecloth, you have not failed as an at-home mom if you've managed to weave a tender heart within your child.

## Goodness

With all the controversy within governments and numbing violence on an overwhelming number of TV stations, your kids will be hard-pressed to find goodness patterned for them. That's where you come in. You and your husband are the first line of defense in defining what is good in your children's eyes.

Philippians 4:8 gives some advice on building moral character: "Finally, brothers, whatever is true, whatever is noble, whatever is right, whatever is pure, whatever is lovely, whatever is admirable—if anything is excellent or praiseworthy—think about such things." Since you'll now be able to more closely monitor what's going into your kid's eyes and ears, channel them toward activities that will foster the gift of goodness in them.

## Faithfulness

"As I look around me at all the moms who choose to work, I fail to understand why they see that choice as one that strengthens their family," says Katy, a schoolteacher. "In working with junior and senior-high youth, I've noticed a huge difference in attitude and development between kids with stay-at-home moms and kids whose parents both work. After watching them interact for an hour or so, I can usually guess which is which."

When a mom puts her career goals on hold for her children's benefit, God will bless her faithfulness to her family. Take a look at Luke 6:38, and apply its words to someone who has devoted herself in this way: "Give, and it will be given to you. A good measure, pressed down, shaken together and running over, will be poured into your lap. For with the measure you use, it will be measured to you."

## Gentleness

"Gentleness and self-control are the two fruits I pray for the most in my life as a mom," says Elaine. "I want a gentle spirit from God and self-control when my kids do something that drives me up the wall."

Ranting dulls the impact of even an important message. Instead of bullying a child into submission, guide with a light touch, which is much more effective. When we forget to be gentle, the resulting harshness taints everything.

"I felt awful. I yelled at Kurtis, and all he was doing was being a normal two-year-old," remembers Erin. "For every decision I have to stop and think, *How would God have me handle this?* When I don't wait, that's when I get myself in trouble by saying the wrong thing and doing the wrong thing."

Which brings us to the next area of expertise for the Spirit—self-control.

> **For every decision I have to think, *How would God have me handle this?***

## Self-Control

Unless your husband makes a lot of money, it does take self-control to become a stay-at-home mom. As I've said before, many women will find that after they deduct the expenses associated with working, they really are not clearing that much money anyway. Others, however, will find they need to tighten their belts even more to make living on one income work, bypassing "the extras" and postponing noncrucial purchases.

Even though she can (and should) take concrete steps to ease her transition back into the workplace later, it is true that Mom is taking a detour for the moment. As she puts her children's needs before her own, the gift of self-control kicks in with a vengeance. But that gift isn't given in vain. Nourishing a strong bond between parent and child builds a family foundation that will hold firm when future emotional storms hit.

"The odds were definitely stacked against our family when I quit," says Debbie, a former chemist. "However, with the grace of God and a lot of cutting back, we have made it work. I don't think everyone would like living the way we do, doing without newer cars and eating at home most of the time, but we haven't minded yet."

Nancy, a nurse, also chose time with her children, Drew and Dani, over things. "I stayed at home with both the kids until they began school and would do it all over again if given the chance. It is quite tempting to earn money and advance up the career ladder, but the kids must come first. All the money in the world cannot replace loving time spent with our children."

Practicing self-control is worth it. "What's more valuable," asks Katy, "the relationship you build with your kids or the extra money brought home each week? Money comes and goes, but relationships last a lifetime."

### Staying Close to the Vine

"The fruits of the Spirit aren't something you muster up," says Bonnie. "They spring up on a tree that's been well-watered. You have to grow your roots deep, and the only way to do that is to spend time in the Word and in prayer.

"When we're so busy, we may plan our days and have formulas set," she continues. "But God may have a completely different schedule in mind. We have to be sensitive and let him direct the day."

Amen.

# 12

............................

# Creativity
on the
Home Front

**W**HEN IT COMES TO ENTERTAINING THE KIDS, YOU DON'T WANT TO find yourself cornered by a child who laments, "I had more fun in daycare!" This is one area where we must persevere!

Fortunately, there are all kinds of activities you can tap into, either interacting with others or just enjoying true quality time between you and your child. Videos can be great, but they should be kept to a bare minimum. Whip up those potential couch potatoes and get moving! Sparking creativity in your children is fun, and you'll enjoy challenging yourself, too.

**Getting a Grip on Hands-On Learning**

"My three-year-old son, Josiah, thinks all moms are artsy," says Alisa, a mom from Cape Girardeau, Missouri. "We don't just play Legos—we construct solid engineering masterpieces. We don't just fool around with store-bought clay—we make our own in the kitchen, adding just the right amount of primary food coloring and learning about sculptures and secondary colors all at the same time. Do you know how hard it is to create an orange Tigger or a purple Eeyore when you only have red, blue and yellow dough? Josiah does.

"He also knows how to put on a two-act play, complete with an overture, an intermission and a spotlight (made from a flashlight). And bedtime stories? Hey, all our characters have different voices, and the next morning, they come to life in a little boy's imagination and take on new adventures in our living room."

As Alisa demonstrates, hands-on learning is an attitude of *I have time to let you try, to help you gather the tools of play, to imagine the world your way.*

### Spotting the Extraordinary in the Ordinary

Sometimes being creative just means taking an everyday object and viewing it through a kid's eyes. I had a garage sale once where I tried unsuccessfully to sell a typewriter. Since we are now in the computer age, my old Selectric didn't pique the interest of any adults, although I thought the price was right and I had it attractively displayed in my "Business" section.

Hour after hour, it sat there. Then I got a brainstorm.

Going in the house, I grabbed a piece of colored typing paper. I took the typewriter, put it down on the floor next to the toys, rolled in the sheet of bright orange paper and plugged it in.

> Everyday items can be instantly transformed into something magical.

The very next car that pulled up had a four-year-old who immediately spotted the typewriter, sat down on the concrete and started playing with the keys. The boy grinned at his mother, who grinned at me. Sold!

What was different? Besides the orange paper—nothing. Except location, location, location—and thinking creatively.

You'd be surprised how many everyday items can be instantly transformed into something magical. I remember throwing out some lace curtains once and then realizing my mistake. Plucking the frilly white material out of the trash, I tossed the curtains in the washer. An hour later my girls had wedding veils.

Being creative doesn't have to be expensive. Donning prom dresses and silver and gold shoes I picked up at garage sales, my girls can perform an awesome rendition of "The Nutcracker," pirouetting around our living room. We keep an overflowing box of dress-up clothes in the kids' playroom. The impromptu costumes outfit children from two to twelve as they mind-travel from the Australian Outback to outer space. Little boys have fun at our house, too, because we've also got construction helmets and boots, cowboy hats and swashbuckler stuff. The same cape my little "Snow White" wears trekking through her imaginary forest works well on "Zorro" as he leaps from behind the toy box to do battle with bandits.

### Indoor Safaris and Fun Buckets
Dressed in our African outfits, we like to go on safari after dark. Armed with flashlights, the girls and I go from room to room, searching for "wildlife" (stuffed animals) perched on curtain rods, peeking out from under beds and hiding behind bookcases. Tossing our captives in sacks, we head back to the "mainland" (the living room), where we set up a circus or a zoo with our imaginary pets.

On days when the weather doesn't cooperate, we drag out our Fun Buckets. You know those decorative tins you hate to part with once the popcorn's gone? Throughout the year we fill them with yarn, buttons, clay, feathers, straws, cookie cutters, paints, foiled paper—anything that could possibly be used to create masterpieces. When it's raining or too hot to play outside, I pop the tops and turn the kids loose.

Another cheap-but-fun idea is to clear the table and grab some cans of shaving cream. Squirt mounds of the squishy white stuff and let little hands make cloud formations, cotton-tailed bunnies or abominable snowmen right in your kitchen.

### The World on a Platter
Since it's not always cost-effective to dine out, we find ways to make eating

at home fun. Try having "McDonald's Night" at your house, complete with homemade "Happy Meals." Let the kids decorate brown paper sacks while you fry up the hamburgers and fries. Make shakes by blending vanilla ice cream and milk. Keep a secret box of inexpensive little toys put away for occasions such as this, slipping one into each decorated bag as their treat.

> **Be sure to get them together with other youngsters so your children won't pine for playmates.**

Even though they missed you, your kids were probably used to playing with lots of other children every day while you were at work. Be sure to get them together with other youngsters for creative activities on a regular basis so your children won't pine for playmates.

Include other families with at-home moms in a "Worldwide Lunch Tour" reminiscent of a progressive dinner. Go from house to house, having one ethnic entree at each location. For example, kids could head to "Mexico" for tacos or nachos, stop by "China" for fried rice or egg rolls and then travel to "France" to enjoy a dessert of jelly-spread crepes. Let your children play host when everyone comes to your home.

**Progress to Fun**

Want to focus on fun instead of food? Turn the progressive dinner into a progressive games party. This would work especially well when all the host families involved live on the same block or just a couple of streets apart. Adults and children alike can form skating or bicycle brigades, decorating tricycles or bikes for the trek to each house.

Some ideas for an out-of-doors progressive games party include:

*Beauty shop.* Have a couple of moms run a sidewalk beauty salon where girls—and boys—can get their faces, nails and hair done in outrageous fashion.

*Birdies on a blanket.* Put several badminton birdies on a blanket held by a large group of children. Bounce the birdies into the sky—then dodge birdies while still holding the blanket. Don't get "pecked" or you're out.

*Blind man's volleyball.* Drape sheets over a volleyball net so the sheets reach to the ground. Then play volleyball as usual, trying to figure out where the ball will be coming from. Younger children do well with nucom, a game similar to volleyball, in which players can catch the ball and throw it from teammate to teammate before tossing it over the net.

*Water obstacle course.* Set up a course that winds through sprinklers and soaker hoses and past friends armed with water balloons and squirt guns.

*Bubble pop.* Play music while preschoolers hop on one foot and try to pop bubbles made with large wands. Square-shaped plastic clothes hangers from infant and toddler clothes make excellent wands. Large amounts of bubbles are easy to make by mixing a half-cup of dish detergent with five cups of water and adding two tablespoons of glycerine (available at a pharmacy).

*Balloon darts.* Kids throw darts at balloons containing funny commands ("Stand on your head," "Kiss the cat," "Tickle your mom," etc.) written on rolled-up slips of paper. Have a few special awards ("You win a candy bar!") scattered throughout.

If there are future construction workers in your pack, try introducing them to umbrella cities. All it takes are some wide-legged chairs, sheets, clothespins and umbrellas (the more umbrellas, the better). Open the umbrellas, set them side by side and drape sheets over the tops. Use the wide-legged chairs as tunnels to get into the city. You won't see the kids again until supper.

### I Think I Can, I Think I Can

To spark your own creative ideas, take advantage of the many resources available to you. Libraries are a natural place to start, with their shelves of parenting books and up-to-date magazines, like *Family Fun, Family Circle, American Girl, Boy's Life, Highlights for Children* and *Sesame Street*.

On the Internet, you'll find a terrific site called Family.Com (http://www.family.com), which posts articles from parenting publications in all fifty states. Organizations like Mothers of Preschoolers (http://www.MOPS.org) and Parents as Teachers (http://www.patnc.org) not only have a presence on the Web, but they also sponsor local chapters throughout the United States, providing handouts to participants on

> # Now you can watch them perform without worrying about comp time!

creative play that spurs emotional and physical development.

Local libraries often sponsor "story time," where preschoolers hear books, watch videos and work on crafts with other kids their age. Scouting programs also offer fun activities presented with a moral base. Consider signing children up for music, sports, art or dance. Now you've got time not only to take them to practices but to watch them perform without worrying about accumulating comp time.

It's true that lessons and sports fees can be hard on a tight budget. If you have a friend who teaches lessons you'd like your kids to have, consider bartering services. Or see if some of your relatives would prefer to give lessons as birthday or Christmas gifts rather than add one more toy to an overflowing playroom.

### Tiny Tool Time

Terry and I seized another opportunity for fun one day as he was stacking wood planks to take to the dump. Watching him wrestle those boards gave me an idea.

"Wait a minute." Grabbing a couple of planks off the back of the truck, I found a hammer and some large nails. Karen, who was a first-grader at the time, transformed instantly into a professional carpenter (under my constant supervision, of course).

After pounding in a few hundred nails, she took a brush and began painting her wooden concoction a variety of colors. That project kept her busy all afternoon, as I cleaned up the garage around her. By suppertime I had a garage we could park in again, and she had a "fabulous" work of art. What it was, I don't know, but it made her happy, and that's what counts.

Even if you may not need a few hundred nails pounded, you can still take advantage of your kids' enthusiasm; let them help where they can with some of those home-improvement projects you swore you'd tackle once you quit work. Paint the den, clean out and wash the car, dig into some dirt.

My husband and I carved out a small garden where our girls are free to plant anything they choose, just to see what it looks like growing. We've had some fun combinations like sunflowers towering over strawberry bushes, and cantaloupe vines winding amongst petunias. It's true our carrots and radishes never make it past two inches long, since little fingers can't seem to resist pulling them up to check their progress. But the girls don't mind, and it makes things easier for that pesky rabbit that likes to chew on our vegetables.

Since we actually spend time at our house now, we're more conscious of the animals that share the premises. I'm not just talking about our cats, who, by the way, love having us around. Our Garfield clones demand food and petting all day long. But I'm enjoying showing the girls how creative God is with nature, too. We had the chance to observe the goings-on in a nest of sparrows last summer.

### A Fine Feathered Family
"That silly bird."

Terry once again removed a half-built nest from the new hanging basket I'd bought the week before. What momma bird was thinking, we couldn't guess. The flowers hung from the eave just inches above our garage doors. Every time I backed out of the garage, her little heart must have nearly jumped out of her feathered chest.

But that sparrow was determined. By the third demolition of her prospective home, we gave up. "What a birdbrain!" We let her go for it.

The next day, there were five new eggs in our flowerpot.

The little brown bird sat among the blossoms while her mate flitted to and from the nest. Sooner than I expected, there were five tiny naked babies. Terry saw them every day as he lowered the basket and carefully watered the thirsty flowers, while trying not to drown the baby birds.

Momma flew to a nearby tree, scolding Terry as he messed with her kids. After he rehung the planter, she swooped back to the nest, admonishing her gangly feather sprouters to ignore us.

A constant cheeping chorus soon sounded from the flowers. Whenever

I'd take a look in the basket, five open mouths greeted me. They were so used to my visits, I guess they expected me to feed them too. Already these kids were ignoring their mother's advice!

I wondered what would happen when the little ones tried to fly. Uh oh. baby no. 1 had a crash landing on the concrete driveway. Terry discreetly disposed of him before Karen and Carrie noticed. Then we discovered baby no. 2 chirping under the car while momma bird frantically told her mate to do something.

This location was not going to work, so we went against everything I've ever been taught about birds. Picking up the wide-eyed youngster, Terry gently set the baby bird back in the nest with his buddies. Then he moved the planter to a tree a few yards away.

Stubby (as my girls named the stubborn baby bird) launched himself a couple more times before he got tired of me putting him back in the nest. Finally, Stubby settled down with his brothers and resumed his open-mouthed position, waiting for Mom.

Watching from the window, Terry, the girls and I each held our breath. Would the parents be able to find their nest? Would they shun the baby we had touched?

There they went. Momma and papa bird tentatively hopped from branch to branch, then burrowed into the dense flowers. What a chorus awaited them!

I loved watching those two sparrows minister to their babies during the short time they spent in our basket. And I think it made me appreciate my own two little Stubbies even more.

Actively observing nature, spurring imagination through costumes and music, linking up with other families for fun and food, drawing on the resources available to you: welcome to creativity on the home front—a mother lode of marvelous memories for you and your children.

# 13

.........................

# Passing On
# a Moral
# Inheritance

**M**OMMY, I LOVE JESUS. HE'S MY FRIEND. I WANT TO INVITE JESUS
into my tummy."

I nearly drove in the ditch as then four-year-old Carrie spoke the gentle
if slightly jumbled declaration. We hadn't even discussed God that morning, except for praying over our waffles!

But as Carrie sat securely buckled in the backseat of our minivan,
unseen wheels were turning in her head. Without preamble she crossed a
religious threshold and with the innocence of a child took hold of her new
Lord's hand.

### Recognizing Teachable Moments

I am so glad I was there when she made her decision! Teachable moments
pop up unannounced in our children's lives. Through chance and circum-
stance, we find ourselves poised to offer the kids wisdom or to discover
insights that they teach us themselves.

It may happen as little ones are splashing in the tub or stretching out on a towel after a giggly run through the sprinkler. Often the special times occur in the quietness following an exciting or upsetting event, before tears have dried and while hearts still pound. You never know where or when the lightning will strike.

My sitter used to report on the flashes of inspiration, the tentative steps taken by my toddler or those tough questions deferred for when "your mother gets home." Invariably the burning inquiry had been forgotten by the time I arrived to pick them up. I'd missed it.

There's no use in crying over spilt milk or faded lightning strikes. I'm here now.

Or am I?

There can be an awful lot of work for an at-home mom—vacuuming sooty carpets, tackling mountains of laundry; comparison shopping and then preparing and cooking purchases for dinner. Dingy shower stalls cry out for scrubbing, and mud-tracked floors demand mopping.

Seasons change, prompting countless trips up and down attic and basement stairs, lugging boxes of various garments to be cleaned, sorted and packed away again.

The phone rings as schools, churches and friends call for promised favors. Errands—planned and spontaneous—take me to the four corners of the earth. Dashing from one duty to the next, I wonder how I ever worked full time plus did all this stuff.

In the midst of the household whirlwind a preschool child sits, patiently waiting for me to pass by again and make my next move on the board game we started a while ago.

As you may have guessed, I'm preaching to myself now. I can't let myself be run ragged by commitments that eat up precious hours previously reserved for my kids. Sometimes, I have to just say no—no to housework, no to school, no to church, even no to my friends. Taking a firm hold on my priorities, I refocus, remembering why I quit work.

> **Taking a firm hold on my priorities, I refocus, remembering why I quit work.**

The number one reason I quit? To spend quality time interacting with and teaching my children, building their character morally and spiritually. Everything else is secondary to this main goal.

## Timing Is Everything

If I truly want to influence these precious carrot-tops, I've got to carve out huge blocks of time for them and them alone. There's a great inheritance to share with Karen and Carrie as we experience these fleeting years together.

The years *are* passing at an amazing rate. As I write this, Karen has just turned nine. My heart jumps as I realize her time at home is half over. It seems she just got here!

I've still got a few years to guide her, though, and I plan to make the most of those teachable moments sprinkled throughout our relationship. If I don't teach her, her culture will. Growing up in the 1960s and 1970s, I swallowed the "I'm okay, you're okay" hook whole. "I may not agree with what you say, but I'll defend to the death your right to say it" sounded pretty good—then.

## I'm Not Okay, and Neither Are They

But as I now look into my daughters' eyes, I feel a deep uneasiness at passing on such a philosophy. I don't want to leave Karen and Carrie a legacy of shifting sand that holds no solid ethical absolutes.

The trouble is, that philosophy is everywhere in our society. As parents, we must focus on ways to develop strong, deeply rooted character in our children, instead of chaff that will burn up under God's intense scrutiny.

Parents can take to heart God's words through David in Psalm 32:8: "I will instruct you and teach you in the way you should go; I will counsel you and watch over you." Listen to the twin messages of this verse. First, God will instruct us as parents and teach us the way we should go; he will counsel

> **I don't want to leave a legacy of shifting sand that holds no solid ethical absolutes.**

us and watch over us. Next, we can take that counsel and turn to our children.

Following God's example, we can instruct our children in the way they should go, counseling and watching over them. We are not alone; God implements a terrific support system that begins with him.

Read this message I received from a mother who had just turned in her resignation:

> I am looking forward to feeling like a "real" mom. Isn't that a crazy thing to say? I know that I am a "real" mom right now, but I spend so little time with my son. I can't imagine continuing on this path, of only seeing him on evenings and weekends. I want to be the most important person in his life, so that when push comes to shove and peer pressure at school starts, he'll have his relationship with his parents as a strong foundation to guide his choices.

It's never too early to start laying the groundwork for passing on our precious moral inheritance. Studies show newborn babies turning toward the sound of their mother's voice moments after birth. Psalm 139:13 describes how God "knit me together in my mother's womb." Isn't it neat to think about that while patting your pregnant belly, singing "Jesus Loves Me" and knowing both God and your baby are listening?

Terry and I refer to Jesus as naturally as if he were sitting right here with us (which, according to the Bible, he is). When something good happens, we say, "Look what God did!" When we pass a wreck on the highway or see someone crying, we ask Jesus to comfort the people involved. When the WWJD ("What Would Jesus Do?") slogan became popular, we got bracelets for our daughters to wear. We'd been training Karen and Carrie for years to ask themselves that very question as they encountered tough decisions.

We've made a conscious effort to surround the girls with activities and acquaintances who encourage them to look at things from God's point of view. Their earliest board books featured Bible characters. Their video library sports VeggieTales and Adventures in Odyssey tapes instead of mystical or horror movies. Songs sung at bedtime tell of God watching over them at night.

Whenever peer pressure continues to exert itself in the form of popular fads that run contrary to God's directives, we explain exactly why God is so hurt (or infuriated) at the practices. We're trying to get Karen and Carrie to take on the mind of Christ, to see things as he does.

Involving children in church activities is a great way to cement the teaching they are getting at home. Make sure the activities—whether sports, music or performance-oriented—are fun and geared toward your child's natural interests. Religious scouting programs are another way to expose children to God's precepts while they're interacting with other youngsters.

When we make God an integral part of every day, the supportive groundwork is set for their own developing relationship with a very personal Savior.

### Sharing the Gospel with Children

Some parents wonder when is the best time to share the plan of salvation with their children. Dr. James Dobson, founder of Focus on the Family, speaks of his conversion experience at age four. My own daughters also accepted Christ when they were very young. But I didn't recognize my own need for a Savior until I was almost sixteen. So how do we know when our kids are ready?

One of the great benefits of being at home and spending so much time with our children is that we are available when they start asking questions about God. We can convey God's Word to them in language they can understand.

> When they start asking questions, we can convey God's Word to children in language they can understand.

Here is the gospel message put in terms a child can understand:

☐ God loves us. "For God so loved the world that he gave his one and only Son [Jesus], that whoever believes in him shall not perish [die] but have eternal life" (John 3:16).

☐ God wants to bless our lives. "I have come that they may have life, and have it to the full" (John 10:10).

☐ But sin (disobeying God) stands in the way.

"For all have sinned and fall short of the glory of God" (Romans 3:23). That means we're not acting the way God wants us to act.

☐ We can't get back on good terms with God by ourselves; we need Jesus to help us. "For it is by grace you have been saved, through faith—and this not from yourselves, it is the gift of God—not by works, so that no one can boast" (Ephesians 2:8-9).

☐ Jesus died for our sins. "But God demonstrates his own love for us in this: While we were still sinners, Christ died for us" (Romans 5:8).

☐ Trusting Jesus is the way to get to God. "For the wages of sin is death, but the gift of God is eternal life in Christ Jesus our Lord" (Romans 6:23). "Therefore, if anyone is in Christ, he is a new creation; the old has gone, the new has come!" (2 Corinthians 5:17). That means we don't have that sin on us anymore, separating us from God.

☐ How do we trust Jesus? We admit we have sinned (been bad), we feel sorry for being bad and we're willing to quit being bad. We tell Jesus we're sorry and ask him to forgive us. "If we confess our sins, he is faithful and just [fair] and will forgive us our sins and purify us from all unrighteousness [make us clean in our hearts]" (1 John 1:9).

☐ Finally, we ask Jesus to become a part of our life and help us to live right and join God's family. "Yet to all who received him, to those who believed in his name, he gave the right to become children of God" (John 1:12).

If your child understands the plan of salvation and wants to trust Jesus as Savior, now is the time to lead them in a simple prayer.

### Nurturing a Childlike Faith

As you encourage your children to deepen their relationship with God, get them their own age-appropriate Bibles, and read the Bible often. Older kids can read on their own and take an active role in family devotions. Christian bookstores offer many good family devotional books. Look for one that includes Scripture memory, and start a memory verse index-card file for each family member, so that verses are not just learned for a day but reviewed often and claimed for a lifetime.

As you begin to read the Bible together, you can point out passages that especially apply to situations they are in right now. Is there a bully in their lives? Read about David and how he stood up to Goliath, even when all his friends turned and ran (1 Samuel 17). Do thunderstorms scare them? Show them where Jesus calmed the storm on the lake (Matthew 8), or where God used a whirlwind to take Elijah up into heaven (2 Kings 2). Do they feel so small that they wonder if God knows who they are? Show them 1 Kings 13:2, where the reign of Josiah was prophesied three hundred years

> **Point out passages that apply to situations they're in now.**

before he took the throne at the age of eight (2 Kings 22:1)!

There's a wonderful peace in knowing your children are safe in God's hands. And if you've never asked Jesus to be your Savior, today could be the day of your salvation, too.

Now that the most important stone is in place, be confident in claiming God's promise to instruct us and teach us as we build this solid moral foundation. Don't feel bad about setting strict guidelines. Boundaries do not trap children; rather, they define safe zones. I am resolved to teach, to tutor, to advocate the tough, honest choices now, while my kids are still receptive to their Momma's insights.

"Train a child in the way he should go," says Proverbs 22:6. I will, and when my daughters make their future decisions, no matter how they choose, they will be able to draw on a moral compass nestled in their hearts.

What better inheritance could I give?

# 14

# When Do I Get Off Work?

GROCERIES BOUGHT. CHECK.

Laundry folded. Check.

Errands run. Check.

Meetings attended. Check.

House spot-cleaned. Check.

Bills paid and checkbook balanced. Check. Check.

Three meals, two squabbles, four baths and a fairy tale later, you collapse on the couch.

It's nine o'clock at night. Do you know where your children are?

That's right. At the top of the banister, staring at you as you stare at the TV. It's a direct violation of International Parent Law.

"What?"

"I can't sleep," announces your fourth-grader, the same one you dynamite out of bed every school morning. "Hey . . . is that popcorn?"

Why do they make us threaten them? "No fair!" he mumbles, plodding back to his room.

"There's an alligator under my bed," wails your preschooler. "And . . .

and . . . " she nervously paces back and forth, "I have to go potty."

"You just went potty."

"I have to go again."

You're tempted to order her back to bed, but the prospect of one more load of laundry today—this time, soiled sheets—prompts you to trot upstairs. As you lean against the bathroom wall, Princess sits on her throne, chattering away to her captive audience.

"Are you done yet?"

"Almost," she smiles.

Short of barricading bedroom doors, does anyone have some ideas on getting children to go to sleep? (Nope, we'd rather not use drugs in their last-snack-of-the-day cookie. Thanks, anyway.)

Hmmm. Maybe we can dock their allowance. ("You lose a dollar if I see you before sunrise!")

Your son lies down but won't get under his covers.

Ah, to have kids who yawn at dinner and snooze by eight o'clock. Do they really exist? Nah, I think that's another fairy tale.

Princess is finally ready to head back to her room. She snuggles between the covers. Kissing her one last time (you hope), you pat her back, close her door . . .

"Not all the way!"

"All right. I'll leave it open a little." You're almost down the hall.

"Mommy . . ." Long pause. A little louder: "Mommy . . ." Pause. *"Mommy!"*

"You rang?"

"Mommy . . ."

"What is it?"

"Mommy . . . I, uh . . ." Squirm. Wiggle.

You're now face to face, illuminated by the Snoopy nightlight. "What?"

She flashes that shy smile that gets you every time. "I love you, Mommy." Soft arms encircle your neck; then she hugs the breath out of you.

She's so cute, you almost forget about that TV program downstairs. "I love you too, Baby. Goodnight."

"'Night, Mom," your son yells, not wanting to be left out.

"Sweet dreams. Now go to sleep."

Heading back downstairs, fatigue sets in again. Switching off the TV, you decide to head for bed yourself. It's been a long day, and it's not even that late yet. But all the days seem to be long since you became a stay-at-home mom. At least when you worked, you got a couple of breaks and an hour lunch where you only had to feed yourself. And when the whistle blew, your boss didn't hop in your car to accompany you home, strapped in his carseat and smearing soggy crackers on the upholstery.

### Letting Them Out of Your Sight

Being a September baby, Carrie just missed the cutoff for kindergarten, since kids in our district had to be five before the first of August. I felt a little sorry for my younger redhead, standing at the window every morning, waving as big sister Karen got on that fabulous yellow bus. Carrie knew in her heart she was missing something great, and she was anxious to get started in elementary school.

So I started checking out preschool programs for her, even though I was perfectly capable of teaching her myself and had been doing so since I quit work when she was a toddler.

Part of me was reluctant to turn her loose, even for two or three half-days a week. But the other part of me was thrilled at the prospect of carving out some regular time for myself.

Am I selfish? I don't think so. A common trait of stay-at-home moms is generosity, a willingness to meet others' needs before their own. But that doesn't mean Mom has no needs at all. Just as we saw in the example that started this chapter, a dedicated stay-at-home mother can find herself drained as she tries to care for her family around the clock with no provision for her own recess. It's important for Mom to enjoy some downtime just as any other full-time worker would, even if her work is done at home.

> Devotion shouldn't translate into deprivation.

You might think there are times in your kids' lives when they are so high-maintenance that it's crazy to let them out of your sight at all. Your newborn is feeding every four hours; your toddler is at the height of exploration fever and needs constant monitoring; the toilet-training isn't going nearly as smoothly as you had hoped; your preschooler is exerting her independence.

But often right in the midst of this juvenile jungle is exactly when breaks between Mom and Junior are needed most. Devotion shouldn't translate into deprivation. A stay-at-home mom needs pockets of time when she can rejuvenate off the clock.

### Making a Break for It

So how do we go about staking out boundaries for Mom's very own free-play zone?

Start by sharing your needs with your husband. He probably already smells the smoke of your impending burnout and is wondering what he can do to help. Tell him.

Love for one's children isn't weighted more for females than their mates, and a dad may even find himself a little envious of the amount of time Mom gets to spend with their kids. So how about setting aside one evening a week as Dad's Night?

As soon as Dad gets home, Mom goes off the clock. Dad takes care of dinner, whether cooking it himself or racing everyone to the minivan, on the way to the local burger joint. He can surprise his kids with a special activity in town, plan some fun at home or just shepherd the kids through their daily nighttime routines of finishing homework and taking baths. Dad enjoys quality time focused on his kids, right up to bedtime stories and tucking them in for the night. These are memories in the making for both a father and his children, who are ecstatic to have Dad all to themselves.

Meanwhile Mom's enjoying a guilt-free, temporary release from responsibility. Just look at all the cool things she can do with a free evening:

☐ visit girlfriends, even some without kids

☐ go shopping for herself without packing a stroller, diaper bag, teething ring, juice cup, etc.

☐ see a movie without animated characters

☐ attend an amusement park without a visit to the nurses' station or glancing at the "You Must Be This Tall to Ride" signs

☐ find a favorite tree, beach or bench and mellow out

☐ order what she wants to eat, with onions, mushrooms or anything else she loves—without having to apologize to anyone

☐ go for a drive on a warm evening with the window down, a soft drink she doesn't have to share in one hand and music *she* likes wafting from the radio

A word to Dad: One important aspect of "Mom's Night Out" is the no-penalty phase. That means the dishes from the dinner she didn't have to cook are washed, the games you and the kids played are put away, and her darlings are bathed and in bed to stay by the time she gets back home. If you now have some special time planned for just the two of you, then you're on track to making the evening a total success.

### I Want to Be Alone

One reason for actively pursuing friendships with other stay-at-home moms is to avoid feeling isolated. Another is to find someone who will help you out when you want to be alone.

> **Set some reasonable boundaries so Mom can continue to thrive in the commitment she's made to her family.**

I have developed close relationships with two other former working moms who also have children close to my daughters' ages. I like these women, and my girls respect them and enjoy playing with their kids. We've shared many activities together, and I feel comfortable with my friends' parenting techniques, which are very similar to mine.

Now that we trust one another, I feel no hesitation in leaving my children under their supervision. Since we barter babysitting with each other, it costs nothing but time. Our kids love it because there just aren't any toys quite as wonderful as the ones at somebody else's house. Funny, but my friends' children feel the same way about the stuff scattered around our place.

Consider trading off an afternoon or morning a week, allowing each woman a window in time to temporarily ease off her titles of mother and wife and just be herself for a little while. Once a month you might even have one mom watch all three sets of kids while the other two go out, rotating who gets to supervise the crowd. It can even be fun when your turn comes to babysit the whole bunch, because the kids are psyched and happy to romp with their buddies.

### In-Town Respite

Besides your husband and friends the community may have some ideas for giving you a break. Local churches often have "mother's day out" programs that invite children to fun activities a couple of days a week while their parent takes a breather for a few hours.

June signals the beginning of Vacation Bible School (VBS) season. VBS classes generally run three hours each morning or a couple of hours at night for five days, and they are free to the community. Just about every church sponsors their own VBS, week-long celebrations where children enjoy activities and treats interwoven with solid moral teaching. Churches normally cater to kids ages four to twelve. Don't miss this great chance to carve out some quality time for yourself while making sure your kids are well supervised and having fun.

I make a point of signing my girls up for two VBSs each summer, besides the one held at our home church, so they have one special series to look forward to each month. This summer they're blasting into outer space, taking part in a tropical island adventure and going on a fishin' mission with Jesus. I carefully select programs at churches where my kids have friends and where I know some of the parents and organizers. The evening VBSs are especially nice for Mom and Dad, because parents can spend some time alone together while the kids are being entertained with crafts and games.

My favorite VBS ever was when Moses visited a church down the block. The theme was the Ten Commandments, and my daughters loved it, especially when the plagues hit. You wouldn't think plagues would be so cool, but they rained down on this youthful congregation in the form of plastic flies, frogs and Styrofoam hailstones. I haven't seen such a free-for-all since our subdivision's garage sale.

In a make-believe wilderness teachers served manna (crackers) and quail (fried chicken), and at the end of the week the kids came home with a sackful of rubber snakes, sugar-cube pyramids and thick plywood tablets handwritten with God's laws. It was great.

### Exploring Preschool

As children get older, preschool provides an opportunity for them to interact with their peers on a regular basis and eases them into the structured routine that comes with kindergarten. I don't believe preschool is essential for all children, but I do know the thought of a couple of mornings a week with other mini-students sounds like heaven to most five-year-olds.

I like the idea, too, because while my child is raising her hand, reciting her ABCs and counting to one hundred, I can find some fun of my own. I might do some favorite crafts, read up on current events or log on to an interesting chatroom. I can write letters to friends or stories to editors. I can enjoy some quiet moments with God. Some days I use the time to catch up on chores to help me feel more focused, but I always reserve some interval for pure relaxation.

By the time my preschooler runs to my arms, waving her fingerpainted masterpiece and chattering happily about her time at school, I'm recharged and ready for fun!

So when you start wondering *When do I get off work?* don't add to your stress by feeling guilty you posed the question. Supermoms at home are just as much of a façade as Superwomen in the workplace. Let friends, family and your community help provide well-deserved breaks while you find some balance in your role as a stay-at-home mom.

# 15

·······················

# Oh, to Hear Another Adult Voice

**I**THINK I'D GO BANANAS TALKING TO NOBODY BUT A TWO-YEAR-OLD ALL day long."

Of course you would. So would I. Even Einstein's mommy must have said, "Gee, this relativity stuff is interesting and all, but frankly, Al, I need a break."

> **We moms need to stick together.**

You're energized and ready to take on this exciting new phase of your life—but a few questions linger.

"I don't know any stay-at-home moms, and I need support. Where do I find other women who have made the same parenting choice I have?"

"I love my child, but sometimes he drives me crazy! Is there something wrong with me?"

"I'm not sure I'm cut out to be a full-time stay-at-home mom."

When we were working outside the home, most of us had other people around to hear our new ideas or ongoing frustrations. Adult companionship is a perk of working life. Stay-at-home moms have an extra challenge to overcome: avoiding the isolation that can easily drive a beleaguered parent to tears.

My own mother is more than willing to give me parenting advice, but she and my dad live four hours away. One of my brothers lives across state; the other is stationed overseas. That's not unusual; our society is so mobile that extended families are often available only through long-distance phone calls, the Internet or periodic visits.

But there's no reason to allow ourselves to become isolated and lonely. There truly is strength in numbers, and we moms need to stick together. Plenty of resources are available via local groups or the Internet. And if there isn't a support group already started in your area, you can always use those great organizational skills of yours to get a new one going.

### Calling In the Cavalry

There are kindred spirits out there you haven't yet met. You're very likely passing them in the aisles of the local discount department store or sitting at the table next to them as you each watch your kids play in the ball pit at McDonald's. As you're taking a stroller walk with your baby, notice other women in your neighborhood who are outside with their children during normal working hours. You've just spotted potential buddies.

**Make friends with other women who share the same commitment to staying home with their children.**

I was surprised to discover that many of the women I associated with through church and extracurricular activities were stay-at-home moms. When a friend and I launched a local play group called "Doing the Mom Thing," we expected five or six ladies to sign up. When fourteen expressed interest, we knew we were on to something.

Choosing low-cost or free activities, we scheduled weekly get-togethers that gave us a reason to get out of the house and interact with each other. Our children loved it, of course, because they got to play with their friends at the park or the zoo or the swimming pool—wherever we decided to go that week. And the moms had a chance to talk and make friends with women who share the same values and commitment to staying at home with their children. It was a win/win situation which stimulated both mother and child. (See chapter twelve, "Creativity on the Home Front," for more ideas on fun outings and activities.)

## This Too Shall Pass

It may be hard to imagine while you're in the midst of toddlermania, but things will get easier as your children grow. The difference between parenting a two-year-old and parenting a five-year-old is dramatic. One obvious change is that most five-year-olds no longer eat checker pieces or marbles. Their moms still stick close by, but we don't have to watch every single movement our child makes, averting disaster in the form of stairs, cleaning fluids or electrical outlets. In short, it's all downhill from here; those pockets of relaxation time will increase. Until the teenage years, at least (or so I'm told—but that's another book!).

So hang in there; it won't always be this crazy. Meanwhile, let's get you some help. At the back of this book is a resource section listing various organizations that have devoted themselves to encouraging and educating full-time and part-time stay-at-home moms. Through local meetings, workshops, magazines, newsletters and Internet websites, these groups form a supportive network.

These resources will help you in your quest to be a terrific stay-at-home mother. But there will also be times when you will want to focus on something completely unrelated to parenting. You shouldn't feel guilty about nurturing personal interests that have nothing to do with crayons or Mr. Potato Head. After all, you've got a lot of different facets to you in addition to your important role as Mommy.

When I worked full-time, I simply didn't have the time to plan for the future or consider what I'd really like to do with my life. Now in those quiet times while my child naps or plays contentedly nearby, I can think about ways to fulfill myself on other levels, too.

### Step Back and Regroup

I believe there should be a healing period for harried, overworked mothers who have just resigned their jobs. In my case, I took six months off from everything but rediscovering my immediate family. I quit committees, resisted overbooking myself with "fun" activities and put off people who figured I could take care of their errands since I wasn't working. As my blood pressure dropped and my stress dissipated, I found it was a great time to take personal inventory.

> Mom can still be there for the big game.

You might consider doing the same. The deadlines are done; the alarms are silenced. Now, what do you really *like* to do? Is there something you're especially good at, a trait that others see in you and praise you for?

When you consider going back to work in the future, does the idea of taking up your old profession energize or demoralize you? If you were to head in a different direction, what training would you need?

Outside of your family, what is important to you? Do you wish you could become more active in your community? Are there any special causes—religious, political, social, etc.—that you would like to support and promote? Is there some skill you would like to learn? Are there friendships you'd like to deepen?

Once you determine an area you want to cultivate, share your ideas with your husband and then begin to schedule activities that nurture Mom. Maybe it's a dance class or sessions with ceramics. It could be courses at the local university or occasional weekend getaways with old college friends. It may be volunteering at the hospital or campaigning for a candidate. Wherever you decide to branch out, choose activities that are personally rewarding but won't overly tax your time or resources.

### The Part-Time Option

There's another avenue you might also consider as you think about carving out some time relating to people taller than your belly button.

Many women find their comfort zone by blending a nondemanding part-time job with their commitment to spend more time with their children. This works especially well for parents whose youngest child has entered school, thereby freeing up several hours a week when the kids won't even notice Mom's gone.

"Both of my children were in school full time last fall," says Diane, a mom from a small midwestern town. "I wouldn't even consider getting a job, because I was certain there were none where you were able to work part-time and still put your family first.

"But I was wrong. Our local library was looking for a page. I applied and got the job. I am able to stay home on sick days, school holidays, snow days, whatever. My boss is wonderful. I have had to take numerous days off, and she has always said my place is with my children. Also, I get summers off. In short, I never have to work if my children are not in school.

"I am able to get out fifteen hours a week, be with adults and still have time for myself. In short, I think I have the dream job."

Instead of feeling guilty about not being a stay-at-home mom in the purest sense of the word, many women find a comfortable balance in piecing together the worlds of career and home-making in the manner Diane has described. With a flexible part-time job such as this the head-to-head conflicts that once caused so much heartache are avoided. Mom can still be there for the special performances, the spelling bees, the big game. But she also maintains some time for herself. Adding a little extra income to the family pot helps too.

> **Home and work mix to form a satisfying scenario for parent and child alike.**

### Establishing a Home-Based Business

Sometimes a woman will have the opportunity to perform a part-time job directly from her home. For many this is an ideal situation, as home and work mix to form a satisfying scenario for parent and child alike.

As I mentioned in chapter six ("How Do I Tell My Boss?"), if you present a detailed plan that spells out benefits to the company, your former employer may be willing to let you work from home. If you find your supervisor is interested in keeping you on the payroll, ask the company to provide necessary equipment you need to perform your job on a part-time basis.

For instance, if you are currently an office worker, your boss may let you move your work computer to your home. If you already have a personal computer but lack the proper software or Internet access for researching or transmitting documents, ask the company to pay for these items.

Joy, a seamstress, had been working at a bridal shop doing alterations. She and her supervisor worked out a compromise to allow Joy to sew at home. The onsite staff would do the measuring and pinning; Joy would pick up the dress, do the work and return it to the shop. "My supervisor and I had worked together for three years, so she knew she could trust my work. And I knew exactly how she wanted the job done. Once you understand how someone works, you can read their signs without talking."

Joy also printed up business cards and left them with local bridal and fabric stores. She figured that even when a shop had an alterations person on staff, there would still be times when an extra set of hands would be needed. She was right.

She soon had a call from a dry cleaning business. "I started doing alterations on a temporary basis, so they could see how they liked my work. It worked into a regular gig."

"I love not having the hassle of having to get up, get ready and then hit rush hour," says Joy. "I much prefer staying home, and if I want to work in my robe that day, I can!"

Janean, an energetic, artistically gifted mom who's caring for her two boys, Taylor and Trenton, has explored many different do-it-yourself options over the years. "I've always done things from inside the home to make money. I've sold Tupperware, Discovery Toys, Herbalife and Creative Memories stuff. I made custom gift baskets and painted murals on customers' baby-room walls while Stace [her husband] watched the boys.

"I ran a preschool program with two employees for twelve kids out of my home for four years. Using my computer, I did desktop publishing, making up newsletters and personalized cards for other in-home daycare centers." Whew! This is one stay-at-home mom you'll never see lounging about eating bonbons.

Business cards, flyers and newspaper ads can be useful in finding clients for your at-home business. Word-of-mouth advertising is invaluable. You might even want to post a small sign in your yard, but be sure to check with your local city government first for any restrictions or required licenses.

### Setting Up a Home Office

☐ Designate a set place where you will perform your business duties, whether it be an extra bedroom, a breakfast nook or a corner of the family room. Decorate the area in a way that makes you feel comfortable and productive, with the tools you need close at hand. Even if you work in the basement, make it as attractive as you can. Paint the walls; put up a picture.

☐ Don't feel that you need all the bells and whistles the first day. I typed my first cover page magazine article on a green-screened computer I'd bought at a garage sale for thirty dollars.

☐ With the advent of desktop publishing, advertising expenses can be minimized. Use a computer to design your own business cards and flyers instead of having a print shop make them up. If you don't have a computer, check out your local library or community college. Often, computer access is available for free or very little cost to the public. Onsite staff can help you familiarize yourself with the equipment.

☐ While you're at the library, take note of books or magazines related to your profession. There's no need to invest money in subscriptions when you can check out magazines and newspapers. Don't be discouraged if you don't see the periodical you want on the shelves. Go to the library system computer and see if another branch carries the magazine you need. If you spot the correct title, ask the librarian to request the materials and have them transferred to your local branch. Still no luck? Check out the library's computerized InfoTrac SearchBank, which contains text from thousands of articles that can be printed out for a nominal fee.

☐ It is not necessary to have a separate business line. Do, however, educate family members in proper phone etiquette. You might want to set certain time spans where only you pick up the phone, say during regular office hours. If you work extensively on the Internet or will tie up the phone line while telemarketing, consider "Call Notes" or another messaging service.

☐ If you can cover the household bills on your husband's salary alone, roll the money you make from your home-based, part-time job back into the business. That way, you can steadily upgrade your equipment and inventory without draining family finances.

☐ Although you will need to set limits on your children's use of your work area, be sure to make them feel welcome. I have a miniature table and chairs next to my desk where my girls can color, read or put together puzzles while I write.

### Discovering Your Niche

All at-home moms are not cut from the same cloth; we're individuals with specific needs, ambitions and abilities. The uniting thread comes in deciding to reprioritize our lives so that our children rank infinitely higher than they did when our sights were set elsewhere.

Whether you decide to be a full-time at-home mom or think the part-time job or home business is the right route for you, continue to keep those kids directly in your sights. If they drop out of view and you find yourself as inaccessible as when you worked outside the home full-time, try a different tack that places less demand on your time and energies. With time, you'll find the right fit for you and your family.

# 16

.........................

# Finding
# Your Mentor

**D**ESPITE BEING VERY EXCITED ABOUT BEING HOME, I AM FEELING unexpectedly grouchy," writes a teacher contemplating her impending last day of work. "I feel stressed about the decision, hoping that I haven't just put my family in financial jeopardy. I also feel like I am about to lose whatever self I have left. My fear is that I am going to spend my whole existence doing for everyone else, and no one will do for me.

"That didn't come out right. What I meant is that [when I am working] I have a definite identity. I am known by the community . . . have a noble sense of purpose and spiritual fulfillment that I am using the natural gifts and talents God gave me. I am afraid that I am going to be cleaning and doing laundry and will lose my sense of self and purpose. Now this sounds irrational; it's probably not true. I will discover a new self, and new gifts and talents will emerge. It's just the transition that's hard. I feel like I'm on one side of the river, and I have to get to the other. Once I'm there, I'll be fine; it's just swimming through the frigid water that makes me leery.

"Was it a hard transition for you? Were you grumpy to your family? I'm trying not to be. I just have to get past my fears."

As this young woman related her feelings so transparently, I understood her hesitancy. I also grasped her need to get advice from someone who had already quit her job to be with her children. No matter how prepared we are, it's still comforting to talk to someone who is living the life toward which we're heading.

## Learning from Others' Experiences

Mentors appear throughout the seasons of our lives, and it is a smart woman who takes advantage of their wisdom. In high school it could have been the coach who believed in your abilities. In college perhaps it was a professor who challenged you to think beyond ordinary logic. On the job she may have appeared as the boss who took you under her wing and taught you to soar in the business world.

You may find it helpful to learn from someone who has blazed a trail you can follow in this arena, too. There's no one stereotypical figure who fits the stay-at-home mom mold. Just like in other professions, women answering this particular calling fall into a variety of different personality traits and strengths, skills and abilities, ethnic and economic categories. Each and every one of them needs support. The trick is linking them up with other like-minded women.

While it is very helpful to visit with moms near your own age, be sure also to talk with older mothers whose children are now grown. They've seen it all, from toddler to teenager, and have great insight on the varied aspects of a stay-at-home mom's life, from budgeting to Band-Aids.

Perhaps most helpful is the mom who's presently in the thick of it, but who's been enjoying her at-home role a few years. You'll get firsthand, up-to-date info on handling the stresses and joys of this precious profession from someone who has not only been there, done that, but is doing it still.

Be direct; ask the tough questions. What's it really like to live on a reduced income? Does your husband respect you as much as he did when you were working outside the home? What are you doing to keep your foot in the door at work, just in case you want to come back after the kids are older?

Find out how she handles that inevitable tough session with the kids. Will twenty-four hours a stretch, week upon week with a toddler turn your mind to mush?

> **Will life with a toddler turn your mind to mush?**

More than likely, what you hear from moms who have gone before you will make you even more anxious to join them. I've been a working mom and I've been a stay-at-home mom. This more relaxed, more focused lifestyle has done wonders for my family and me. Although it definitely is not for everyone, the at-home lifestyle definitely *is* for me!

## Homebodies

From my home office I write a newspaper column called "Homebodies" that I also e-mail over the Internet to moms from Maryland to Korea. Contact me at cgochnau@sky.net and you can begin receiving this free newsletter. I can't tell you how gratifying it is to receive responses from readers like this one:

"I started reading your column two years ago, when my son, Matt, was just born. Reading it on a regular basis really helped my husband and me set priorities, and we set out to put me in a position to quit work. It really affirmed to me that it is okay to quit that career—the seeming pinnacle of a woman's life, at least according to modern society. That it was okay to live a simple life and reject the 'keep up with the Joneses' business. That even if I bought clothes on sale or shoes at a discount store, these things were just no big deal.

> **It's okay to live a simple life and reject the "keep up with the Joneses" business.**

"We have friends that take cruises, live in big four-bedroom houses, have vacation homes . . . on and on. But my treasure is the light in my two-year-old's eyes, and the peace and tranquillity that my family will feel when we all aren't scrambling to do all the chores during the four precious evening hours that we're home together.

"Your column helped encourage me to figure out what I really wanted out of life, and I appreciate that. Just one more thought—I've often wondered if it wouldn't be good to target younger women who are getting married, to get them thinking ahead. I know that if I had known earlier that I wanted to stay at home when we had children, we would have made different financial decisions earlier in our marriage. It wouldn't have taken us years to put ourselves in the position we are in now."

Do you see how, even as she's thanking me for helping her, this reader is revealing her own gift for mentoring? Look at her concern for keeping other women from falling into the financial trap from which she and her husband had to extricate themselves before she could quit work. She has the makings of a mentor, and she's just getting started.

### Finding a Like-minded Confidant

If you want to find a mentor, go where other stay-at-home moms go. As you read in chapter fifteen ("Oh, to Hear Another Adult Voice") and can see in the appendix at the back of this book, there are a growing number of organizations dedicated to encouraging stay-at-home moms. Getting involved with a couple of these groups puts you in touch with other women who can be great resources for you. Be sure to give it some time; more than likely it'll take a few meetings before you begin to feel comfortable enough to really open up. Or you may get lucky and meet a soulmate right off the bat.

> You may get lucky and meet a soulmate right off the bat.

You'll find traditional ways of meeting other at-home women still work well, too. Volunteer to be a room mother at your child's school or a den mother of her scouting troop. Attend the women's Bible study at church, or join your church's Vacation Bible School committee and teach your son's class. If you are politically active, interact with other moms who are daytime volunteers for your favorite cause or candidate.

As you get to know the other women in your chosen group, there will probably be one or two that you especially click with. Develop personal friendships that go beyond the scope of the weekly meeting with these moms. Share experiences and exchange phone numbers—you never know when you might need to dial them up. After all, one of *those* days might be right around the corner.

You know what I mean. By this point in this book you know I love my girls, but that doesn't mean I've never gone head to head with them.

Psychologists warn about the turbulent years a decade ahead, but sometimes I think kids get their teenage basic training in a boot camp called Toddlerhood.

Why do these little guys act like Pavlov's dog when the phone rings? They need a drink and they need it now. And must they wind themselves so tightly in the twenty-five-foot extension cord while Mom struggles to finish her conversation before the line goes dead?

One of the best inventions ever developed is the portable phone. Now we can at least hide in a locked bathroom to talk, although tiny fingers still probe under the door as incessant knocking and "whatcha doings" threaten to drown out the caller.

Tell me why some three-year-olds are determined to wear their shorts in December and parkas in July—and will scream and throw themselves on the floor if we don't let them play in the snow in their sandals.

And why—please answer this one for the sake of my sanity—is there only *one* doll that will enable my child to sleep tonight, and that idolized Barbie is nowhere to be found? (Goldilocks has probably bribed Ken to take her away from all this and is out cruising in her Mustang convertible.)

Just like the classic werewolf movies, on trying days we can steadily morph from sweet mother to raging maniac, terrorizing the countryside. You'll be glad you've got someone to talk with the next time you feel the Stay-at-Home Momster emerging because your toddler is acting his age: picking flowers for you (out of the neighbor's garden), refusing to eat anything but jellybeans today (yesterday it was pickles) or trying out his freehand drawing (with permanent markers on your guest bathroom wall).

Pick up the phone and call your prearranged soulmate who has given you permission to periodically vent your frustrations. Dump all over her! Believe me, you will feel better, and she'll be relieved to have someone she can call when she feels her own inner Jekyll leaning toward Hyde. Guess what—she's probably got some advice you would have thought of yourself on a more levelheaded day. Take that insight, get a cool drink of water, and approach your children with a new plan in hand. You'll be able to keep that Stay-at-Home Momster at bay, even when there's a full Moon Pie ground into your carpet.

### Blessings from One Mom to Another

We never outgrow our need for an understanding listener to pump us up on bad days or a cheerleader who celebrates our wonderful times with us. Posted on the wall by my desk is an encouraging note written to me by one of my own mentors. When I sense stress lurking at my door, I take a look at this dear friend's words and let them rejuvenate me:

A stay-at-home mom is more likely to be tuned in to her family, and because of that:

☐ maybe she'll catch a behavioral problem in her son before it gets out of control

☐ maybe she'll have more time to talk to her teenage daughter, strengthening family ties, and keeping her from getting in with the wrong crowd

☐ maybe she can volunteer more at her kid's school, and thus encourage a weary teacher

☐ maybe she can greet her kids upon their arrival home from school, preventing them from viewing trashy talk shows, soap operas, or violent cartoons

☐ maybe she can prepare a clean and welcoming environment for them to de-stress in after school

☐ maybe other kids will view her as accessible and share concerns with her that might otherwise go unnoticed by workaholic moms

☐ maybe she'll be more available to help her aging parents, as needed

☐ maybe she'll have greater physical and emotional resources to deal with marital demands, not to mention time for a nap in the afternoon so she won't hop into bed that night with nothing but sleep on her mind

☐ maybe she'll live longer and have more blessings in heaven

There's no doubt she'll have more blessings here on earth.

# 17

·························

# Developing a Personal Mission Statement

**A**S I WRESTLED WITH AN OVERLOADED BASKET OF LAUNDRY, I SPOTTED my mother in the full-length mirror at the end of the hall, struggling toward me with the same burden. Seeing as Mom lives a couple hundred miles away, in an instant I flashed from surprise to recognition of my own reflection.

When she was my age, my mother was raising three strong-willed teenagers. Fast-forwarding to the present, I'm now parenting a couple of lively elementary-age kids. But Mom's long-ago desires and mine are the same: to somehow create a safe and nurturing place for our family.

> I want to influence their lives for good.

It's funny. I thought Mom thought she had it all under control. Now I know—she was constantly in a state of resolution, trying to live up to her own personal goals for her family. All mothers are, whether they're just starting out or are already helping dye their own daughter's hair.

There are so many things I want to do for my children; so many ways I want to influence their lives for good. To help keep me focused, I came up with a mission statement for my family, which reads:

"To create a secure and happy home where my children can flourish spiritually, physically, mentally and socially as I love, teach and encourage them. I'll give them the top spot in my list of priorities, right after cultivating my relationships with God and my husband."

Putting resolutions down on paper seems to strengthen them. There they are in black and white, kind of a touchstone to hold on to when the twister of day-to-day living whirls through the house. So as an addendum of sorts I thought about ways I could reach the goals I'd set in my mission statement and then wrote them down.

### Kids, I Hereby Resolve To . . .

☐ Catch your eye with a smile and a wink; to prove I love you every day.

☐ Notice good stuff on your report card first, bad stuff second, and grade it all in perspective.

☐ Be affectionate with Daddy in your presence so you can learn how to treat your own mate someday. I'll not hide minor disagreements, but I will avoid being petty so you can learn how to work through conflict while maintaining another person's dignity.

☐ Encourage you to spend time with your sister, even if there is a gap in your ages. We'll discover activities you can enjoy together, and I'll treat you in such a manner that you'll realize you're both my favorite daughter.

☐ Resist trying to "fix" all your problems. Instead I'll give insight on possible actions you might take by asking you questions you can answer yourself.

☐ Treat you so you never doubt my love for you, even when I am disciplining you. I will speak well of you in public and never intentionally humiliate you.

☐ Praise but not flatter you, and thereby build in you a fair sense of your abilities. We'll work together to temper any perceived weaknesses and pursue your known strengths so that this time next year, you'll be that much more rooted as you look toward future plans.

**For My Spouse I Resolve To . . .**

☐ Make time to freshen up, both physically and mentally, half an hour before we get together after our respective work, whether inside or outside the home, each day.

☐ Monitor your nonverbal signals and avoid being "chatty" if you're not. I'll let you finish your story of what happened at work without interrupting with my own day's crisis.

☐ Resist asking you to fix anything until after dessert. Unless it's leaking. Or smoking.

☐ Spend an evening each week talking alone with you, whether away from home or relaxing while the kids are out at an activity or with a sitter. I'll also encourage you to carve out occasional getaways with each child, where she can have you all to herself.

> My children are not the product of some cosmic collision but an inheritance from you.

☐ Encourage you to develop close friendships with other men who share your moral values and treasure their families.

☐ Tell you every day that I love you and prove it in action and in word.

☐ Remember you'll be here long after the kids are gone, so our relationship is the most important one under this roof.

**In My Relationship with God I Resolve To . . .**

☐ Remember that my children are not the product of some cosmic collision but an inheritance from you.

☐ Honor your name in my household, so that my kids will get a glimpse of how wonderful you are and want to find out more for themselves.

☐ Obey you, thereby teaching my children how to bend to meet the will of someone who wants only the best for them.

☐ Thank you for everything you've given our family and everything you've kept from us.

☐ Rest in you, as we learn to live more on less.

**And for Myself I Hereby Resolve To . . .**

☐ Do what I can and guiltlessly let the rest wait. I'll try to be content in whatever circumstances I happen to be.

☐ Strive to be the best thing that happened in someone's life today.

☐ Keep everything in perspective and not overreact. Unless it's leaking. Or smoking.

☐ Accept the love of family and friends, and reflect it right back.

☐ Plant happy memories in my children's thoughts, and water them daily with encouragement and humor.

**Recognizing God's Voice**

So what about you? If it isn't God's plan to have every mother stay home with her children, how do you know whether you are one of those being called?

"I have always been a *Little House on the Prairie* fan and wanted that type of picturesque life," says another Web mom, posting her thoughts on a messageboard. "I began reading 'tightwad' books and cut out all the things that didn't add value to my life. I've found I now make saner choices. It is about spending time, not money, and using your head."

"I became a parent because I wanted to raise my children, not give them to someone else to raise," says Pam, who also logged on to share her thoughts. "I consider it my career. I also like being able to give them a happy childhood—what a great thing to be able to give someone!"

"I came to the conclusion that I really needed and wanted to be home with my child," says Shauna. "Although I had a superb babysitter who was like my angel from heaven (she really loves my son), and I had many days off during the year that most working moms don't have, I ached to be at home. I have my entire life to teach, and once my kids are in school full time, a teaching career blends wonderfully with their schedule."

Kim, who has a psychology background, posted her perspective: "Since staying home full time I have been told by my husband repeatedly that his job advancements are due to both of our hard work. He hasn't had to worry about sick children or daycare problems. He says he has a new sense of security knowing that I am taking care of the home and the children.

"He even got a tear in his eye the first time he asked for something from the store and it was there waiting for him when he got home from work," Kim laughs. "Prior to my being home, it would take a week to get anything from the store, since it had to be fit into my already-busy schedule. He likes being my top priority now, along with our children.

"His career really did take off once I stayed home, so I think that our long work-related talks at night and on weekends do help. He has the paycheck, but I am his money manager. I often see a solution to a problem at work that he is too close to. He gets the work promotions and the acclaim, but we celebrate *our* success. Having a former professional at home is his secret weapon!"

### A Steadying Influence

Are you the perfect secret weapon to aid your husband in finding balance and happiness as you help deflect daily stresses? Are you the best teacher your child will ever encounter? Do you have a deep assurance in your heart as you contemplate, and then take steps toward, becoming an at-home mom?

> God has his own personal mission statement he's fulfilling in the lives of our children.

Even though I've been traveling this road for several years now, God still gives me affirmations along the way. They're little checkpoints, keeping me on track and letting me know it's not quite time yet to merge back into my former role outside the home. Here's one of the verses that jumped out at me recently as I listened to our pastor speak, with Carrie sitting at my feet coloring on the bulletin:

> Whatever you do, work at it with all your heart, as working for the Lord, not for men, since you know that you will receive an inheritance from the Lord as a reward. (Colossians 3:23-24)

Part of that inheritance, I'm sure, is the peace that comes from knowing we have done all we could to raise our children right. As one of the fathers I interviewed jokingly said, "Even if they go bad, at least I can say I did everything I could!" He doesn't have to worry; his kids and his stay-at-home wife are doing great—as most people do when they're made to feel loved and important.

"Commit to the LORD whatever you do, and your plans will succeed" (Proverbs 16:3). That's it, isn't it? As my truck-driving husband, Terry, likes to say, that's where the rubber meets the road. Dedicate your future to God, and watch where he takes you.

If you're convinced he's directing you home, start getting yourself ready and expectantly observe how things smooth out. With your husband's support prepare a personalized family business plan. Start brainstorming about how you can use your degree and training on the home front. Lay the groundwork for returning to your career later, if you so desire. Begin bringing those finances in line, but don't obsess over them. Instead, think about what Jesus said in Luke 12:27-31, applying his words to a woman who is answering his nudging to become a stay-at-home mom:

> Consider how the lilies grow. They do not labor or spin. Yet I tell you, not even Solomon in all his splendor was dressed like one of these. If that is how God clothes the grass of the field, which is here today, and tomorrow is thrown into the fire, how much more will he clothe you. . . . And do not set your heart on what you will eat or drink; do not worry about it. For the pagan world runs after all such things, and your Father knows that you need them. But seek his kingdom, and these things will be given to you as well.

Approach your boss and relatives with the quiet confidence that comes from knowing you're making the right decision. Keep upbeat and productive as you interact with coworkers right up to your last day. Once you resign, enjoy exploring all the ways you can spark creativity in your children and yourself.

Let God empower you with his spiritual gifts of love, joy, peace, patience, kindness, goodness, faithfulness, gentleness and self-control as you approach each day. Link up with kindred souls who have also decided to take time out from their careers to raise their children. Encourage other moms, and allow yourself to be encouraged. Find a mentor whose advice you trust.

As time passes, periodically review your situation and see if you're still on track to accomplish the goals you and your husband have set for your family. Be flexible. But most of all, listen to God. Acts 17:26 says, "And he determined the times set for them and the exact places where they should live." If you think about it, that's an awesome statement. Each life is so important to God that he waited for exactly the right time and place for your baby to be born. And he chose you to be the mother of this particular child, backing you up with all his resources as you tackle this most amazing of all jobs—shaping another person's life for good.

God knows just where he's going to use our babies in his historical time line, saying, "I know the plans I have for you . . . plans to give you hope and a future" (Jeremiah 29:11). In effect, he's got his own personal mission statement he's fulfilling in the lives of our children.

When I get quiet, I can hear it—that famous still, small voice. For me it wasn't in the whirlwind of a working mom's hectic schedule, in the rumbling earthquake of office politics and backstabbing jealousies or in the status-seeking fire that consumes so many as they gather possessions instead of memories. I heard the first whisper as I rocked gently in my recliner with my baby at my breast, my precious child's eyes looking into mine with an unguarded trust.

*This is the exact time for me to be a mom, and home is the exact place where I should be.*

Are you supposed to be home too? Listen and see what he says.

# Appendix

......................

## Resources
## for Mom

ONE OF THE MOST POPULAR PARENTING ORGANIZATIONS, MOTHERS of Preschoolers (MOPS) encourages all mothers to be the best moms they can be. Over eighty thousand women participate in two thousand groups meeting September through May in churches around the world. At these regular get-togethers moms are equipped for the responsibilities of family and community. They explore areas of creativity and express their thoughts and frustrations freely in discussion groups. Kids are instructed in the onsite MOPPETS program while their mothers spend some time interacting with other like-minded friends. Fees and meeting schedules are determined by local groups.

*MomSense,* the bimonthly newsletter for MOPS members, says its purpose is to "nurture the general audience of mothers of preschoolers with articles that inform, entertain and give a balanced perspective on issues of interest and the application of biblical principles to everyday life." MOPS's online website (located at http://www.MOPS.org) features a useful "Tip for the Day" and a daily two-minute radio vignette (also called "MomSense") hosted by MOPS president Elisa Morgan airs on hundreds of stations. Check with your local Christian radio station to see if this MOPS radio program is available in your area.

If there isn't a MOPS group in your town, you might want to consider starting one. You can contact them for this and other information at MOPS International, P.O. Box 102200, Denver, CO 80250-2200; phone (303) 733-5353; fax (303) 733-5770.

Another helpful organization is Formerly Employed Mothers at the Leading Edge (FEMALE). FEMALE's more than six thousand members span North America, sponsoring biweekly meetings and activities sure to "get your brain cells back in gear." Modest membership dues entitle moms to a monthly newsletter and attendance at local meetings featuring topical discussion groups, guest speakers and book discussions. Activities include play groups, family outings and "Mom's Night Out" parties. Babysitting co-ops, advocacy programs and membership directories strengthen the link between at-home moms.

FEMALE's online website at http://FEMALEhome.org/home.htm is packed with information including recent media articles relating to stay-at-home moms and detailed instructions for starting up a FEMALE chapter in your area. You can reach this organization by writing FEMALE, P.O. Box 31, Elmhurst, IL 60126; calling (800) 223-9399; or through e-mail, FEMALEOFC@FEMALEhome.org

Mothers at Home (MAH), a national not-for-profit organization, has been dedicated to encouraging stay-at-home moms since 1984, when its three founders decided to form a group to "provide support and encouragement to today's at-home mothers, correct society's misconceptions and refute stereotypes about at-home mothers." Today, MAH continues to spread the philosophy that "motherhood is a remarkable gift, a stage of life to be embraced and celebrated."

MAH's award-winning monthly publication *Welcome Home* is written for and by at-home mothers. Its website at http://www.mah.org is a good resource for any woman who wants to get active in promoting the at-home lifestyle. For more information, or to subscribe to *Welcome Home,* write Mothers at Home, 8310A Old Courthouse Road, Vienna, VA 22182; phone (800) 783-4666 or (703) 827-5903; or e-mail mah@mah.org

The National Association of At-Home Mothers (NAAHM) offers complete support for the at-home motherhood lifestyle, including a quarterly magazine called *At-Home Mother* as well as numerous other member benefits. (NAAHM) is "committed to finding solutions to all of your at-home mothering concerns." Membership is $18 per year.

Some topics covered in NAAHM's *At-Home Mothers' Info Guides* include "How to Start a 'Mommy's Time' Co-op in Your Area," "Choosing the Right Home Business for You and Your Family" and "How to Get the Support and Understanding You Need for At-Home Mothering from Friends and Family."

You can get more information by writing the National Association of At-Home Mothers, 406 E. Buchanan Ave., Fairfield, IA 52556 (e-mail, ahmrc@lisco.com). Also take a look at their comprehensive website (http://www.AtHomeMothers.com), which offers free information, sample articles and *Info Guides,* a bookstore of publications chosen specifically for at-home mothers, and much more.

Hearts at Home, founded by Jill Savage, has been serving stay-at-home moms since 1994. With the vision of professionalizing motherhood, Hearts at Home conferences feature workshops on a variety of topics sure to encourage and equip women focused on the homefront. Conferences are available in several states.

Moms unable to attend the annual conferences can buy home conference packets that include speaker tapes, handouts and other helpful information. The website at www.hearts-at-home.org provides interaction opportunities in the form of bulletin boards and live chats.

Publications include a monthly magazine available for $15 a year and a monthly devotional available for $20 a year. Sample issues of both publications can be purchased for $2. The organization also offers resources to assist mothers' groups. For conference or resource information contact Hearts at Home, 900 W. College Avenue, Normal, IL 61761, or phone (309) 888-MOMS.

*WAHM,* the online newsletter for Work-at-Home Mothers, presents themselves this way: "Is every day at your office 'Take Our Daughters to Work Day'? Are there Legos under your desk? Is your coffee pot the most used appliance in your home? Then you're a WAHM, and this is your magazine." Cheryl Demas is the editor of this lighthearted weekly publication (found at http://www.wahm.com). Demas's website is also available in Spanish.

WAHM provides advice and chat forums, as well as an online bookstore, classified ads and links to other work-at-home moms through WAHM's business directory. The site is part of a web ring that allows easy access to a whole cyberspace community of moms working at home. If you don't have access to the Internet, you may still be interested in their monthly print newsletter. It is available by yearly subscription. For more information, write Maricle Software, Box 366, Folsom, CA 95763, or call (800) ▮▮▮▮▮▮▮▮.

*Proverbs 31 Homemaker* features a monthly newsletter, an Internet website (http://www.proverbs31.org) and "encouragement group" packets designed to help you start your own local support group with a spiritual base. Topics discussed tie into the theme of the godly mother described in Proverbs 31:10-31, as women strive to improve their relationships with Christ, their husbands and their families.

The Proverbs 31 encouragement groups started in Charlotte, North Carolina, in September 1995, and are expanding across the United States. The group's daily two-and-a-half-minute radio show airs on Christian radio stations Monday through Friday. You can write Proverbs 31 Ministry, P.O. Box 17155, Charlotte, NC 28227, or call (704) 849-2270 for more information.

If you're the parent of a school-aged child, you'll want to know about Moms in Touch (MIT). MIT is an international organization that sponsors groups made up of two or more women who meet for an hour once a week to pray for a specific school. Following the guidelines of a loosely structured handbook available through MIT, women use praise, confession, thanksgiving and intercession as they specifically ask God to bless their kids during the hours they are in school.

"It's crucial to pray for our children, to keep them in God's hands," says Suzanne, an at-home mother who meets each week with another mom with kids at the same school. "Plus, we pray for the buses, the teachers, the safety of the building and about the curriculum. It helps keep us focused on staying involved with our kids' schools."

Lamentations 2:19 sums up the goal of MIT: "Pour out your heart like water in the presence of the Lord. Lift up your hands to him for the lives of your children." You can find Moms in Touch on the worldwide web (http://www.europa.com/~philhow/moms_in_touch.html). Their snail mail address is Moms In Touch International, P.O. Box 1120, Poway, CA 92074-1120. The phone number is (800) 949-MOMS.

*The Dollar Stretcher,* while not specifically a publication for stay-at-home moms, is a good source of cost-cutting ideas. Publisher Gary Foreman's online newsletter, subtitled *Your Weekly Resource for Simple Living,* can be accessed on the Internet (http://www.stretcher.com). *Dollar Stretcher* columnists give frugal advice on topics like gardening, home repair and car care, while articles tackle projects like throwing terrific parties on a budget.

You might consider joining the more than thirty-three thousand families who receive Foreman's free weekly e-mail newsletter featuring money-saving ideas and tips from *Dollar Stretcher* readers around the world. An additional monthly print version contains information that will not be made available online. You can get a sample issue of the print version for $2 by e-mailing Foreman at gary@stretcher.com or by writing him at *The Dollar Stretcher,* P.O. Box 23785, Ft. Lauderdale, FL 33307.

Finally, I'd like to encourage you to contact me personally at (cgochnau@sky.net), so I can add your e-mail address to the list of subscribers to my weekly *Homebodies* newsletter. It's free, and I'm always looking for feedback from moms like you so we can help other women struggling with—or celebrating!—the experiences of the stay-at-home mother.

You can also visit my website at www.homebodies.org or write me at P.O. Box 6883, Lee's Summit, MO 64064-6883.

**Other Suggested Reading**

Burkett, Larry. *Women Leaving the Workplace.* Chicago: Moody Press, 1995.

Hunter, Brenda. *The Many Sides of a Woman's Heart.* New York: Galahad, 1997.

Morgan, Elisa, and Carol Kuykendall. *What Every Mother Needs.* Grand Rapids, Mich.: Zondervan, 1995.

Tolliver, Cindy. *At-Home Motherhood.* San Jose, Calif.: Resource Publications, 1994.

Yorkey, Mike. *Saving Money Any Way You Can: How to Become a Frugal Family.* Ann Arbor, Mich.: Servant, 1994.